Jacob's Journey

Jacob's Journey

Escape from Communist Russia

Herb H. Neufeld, Ed.D.

Note for Librarians: A cataloguing record for this book is available from Library and
Archives Canada at www.collectionscanada.ca/amicus/index-e.html

ISBN 1-4120-8432-6

*Printed in Victoria, BC, Canada. Printed on paper with minimum 30% recycled fibre. Trafford's print
shop runs on "green energy" from solar, wind and other environmentally-friendly power sources.*

Offices in Canada, USA, Ireland and UK

This book was published *on-demand* in cooperation with Trafford Publishing.
On-demand publishing is a unique process and service of making a book available for
retail sale to the public taking advantage of on-demand manufacturing and Internet
marketing. On-demand publishing includes promotions, retail sales, manufacturing,
order fulfilment, accounting and collecting royalties on behalf of the author.

Book sales for North America and international:
Trafford Publishing, 6E–2333 Government St.,
Victoria, BC V8T 4P4 CANADA
phone 250 383 6864 (toll-free 1 888 232 4444)
fax 250 383 6804; email to orders@trafford.com

Book sales in Europe:
Trafford Publishing (UK) Limited, 9 Park End Street, 2nd Floor
Oxford, UK OX1 1HH UNITED KINGDOM
phone 44 (0)1865 722 113 (local rate 0845 230 9601)
facsimile 44 (0)1865 722 868; info.uk@trafford.com

Order online at:
trafford.com/06-0187

10 9 8 7 6 5 4 3 2

To my brothers and sisters:
Marie
Jake
Corney
John
Henry
Helen
Frank
Bill
Dave
Abe
Herman

Acknowledgments

I feel obliged to express my thanks to my father and mother for their indomitable spirit and faith in God. My mother, Helena, was responsible for keeping my head on straight and it was she who told me most of the stories concerning the incredible journey to America.

Appreciation is expressed to my older brothers and sister, Helen, who helped fill in the gaps and provide additional insight into the family's past.

To Joyce, my devoted wife and friend, I owe my appreciation for her assistance, support and encouragement. To our daughter, Patricia, and our sons, Michael and Scott, I owe a debt of gratitude for their love, patience and understanding.

To Dr. Eva Shaw I extend my heartfelt and sincere thanks. Her encouragement, professional guidance and support provided the motivation I needed to make the story a reality.

> "Yea, though I walk through the valley of the shadow of
> death, I will fear no evil, for you are with me; your rod
> and your staff, they comfort me."
> —Psalm 23:4

Introduction

Jacob and Helena Neufeld were staunch German Mennonites who endured almost unbelievable conditions in the Soviet Union. They were intimidated, threatened, tormented, starved and abandoned to freeze to death in the wastelands of Siberia. Their greatest fear resulted from the impact of the Communist Revolution, which promised to annihilate Christianity and church-going believers throughout the Soviet Union.

For Jacob and Helena, there could be only one goal in mind: to escape from Russia and, perhaps, one day, to reach the United States of America. Many obstacles, trials and tribulations stood in their way, but somehow, their faith carried them through.

Jacob and Helena were the parents of eleven boys and three girls, all of whom, except two, were born in Siberia before, during and after the Bolshevik Revolution. The family members were peace-loving grain farmers who preferred to be isolated from urban centers and influences. Their desire was to serve God, to be obedient to His word and to live and let live. It was not to be so.

Born in the United States, the thirteenth child and the tenth son, I grew up hearing the stories: the narrow escapes, the numerous threats, the great flood, the starvation and the river of "glass." I was fascinated by the stories that Jacob and Helena told. I trembled when hearing about the constant quest for survival. I shared in the grief expressed in the loss of Marie, my older sister, whom I never saw, except in a photograph.

My older brothers actually took part in many of the events which Jacob and Helena described. During mealtime, when we were all together at the table, my brothers would reveal, incident by incident, the hardships and the close calls they had endured while living in Siberia and eventually escaping to China.

As a young boy growing up on a farm in Madera, California, I made every attempt possible to glean these family stories, to remember as much as possible and to seal them in my heart as well as in my memory. This story is my recollection of what I heard.

Every effort was made to keep the account as close to reality as possible. All of the impressions and descriptions are my own and someone else might have sketched them differently. I have heard some variance of individual events, but I have tried to portray, as accurately as possible, the story as told by my parents and my older brothers and sister.

In order to provide for continuity and interpretation, I have created necessary dialogues from memory and from brief accounts written by my father and mother. Any interpretation of character is my own.

Jacob's Journey

I

Jacob Peter Neufeld was born in 1856, in the small village of Sparrau, in what was then called South Russia. Today, it is known as Dolgoye, in the Ukraine. Because his father, Peter Neufeld, was a blacksmith, Jacob was trained at a young age to forge metal into various shapes and sizes and to build sturdy wagons with iron and wooden wheels.

Sparrau was located in what was called the Molotschna Colony, which consisted of many German immigrants who had moved to Russia at the invitation of the Czars and had settled there since the seventeenth and eighteenth centuries. Many German, Dutch and other ethnic groups had emigrated to Russia to seek new land and to maintain their religious independence from outside influences. The Czars were hopeful that German farmers would migrate to Russia and teach the Russian peasants how to farm.

The good intentions of the plan never materialized. During the 1870s, many Russians became disenchanted and resentful of the Germans who had successfully raised crops and become quite wealthy in their own right. The cultural gap and religious differences did nothing to promote a cooperative venture with the Russians. The Germans were religious separatists who avoided close relationships with other ethnic groups.

When Jacob was twenty-one, he married Ranatha Martens, a neighborhood girl who had also grown up in

Sparrau. Ranatha knew that Jacob had learned the blacksmith trade and that he would be able to provide well for his family. He was a stout, barrel-chested, 250-pound man with a moustache and beard, which fit right in with the accepted look of the Ukrainian day. Their marriage in 1877 produced one son and four daughters.

Ranatha became very ill during the 1890s, suffering from various unknown internal disorders. A doctor was summoned, but was not able to diagnose her correctly. Eventually it was determined that she had some form of cancer, which caused her to suffer great pain for a number of years before passing away in 1905. Although Jacob was grief-stricken at the loss of his much-loved wife, his first concern was for the welfare of his five children. Fortunately, at the time of their mother's death, several of the children were old enough to assume responsibility for the younger ones. Others were placed in nearby homes where they were required to work for their room and board.

Many times during Ranatha's illness, ladies from the church spent time at the Neufeld home cleaning, cooking and helping care for the children in addition to their own duties.

One of the younger girls who volunteered to help at the Neufeld home was Helena Giesbrecht, an eighteen-year-old who knew what it was like to grow up in a family without a mother.

Helena was born in 1886, in Ladekopp, a German village in the northwestern section of the Molotschna Colony. When she was ten, her family moved to a new settlement called Orenburg. She stated in her diary, "On the way to Orenburg, my parents were robbed, so that when we arrived, we had nothing but the wagon and the two horses that pulled it."

Because of their poor circumstances, her father decided to find a place where Helena could stay. She was placed with a family who agreed to give her food, lodging, and about seventy-five cents a month. In exchange for this she was expected to milk four cows both morning and evening and gather hay in the field, putting in as many hours as the adult workers. When she returned to the house late in the evening, her dinner would consist mainly of leftovers from the family table, after which she had to wash the dishes and clean the kitchen.

Sunday soon became a special day for Helena, because as she worked at the assigned daily chores, she began to hear beautiful music coming from somewhere in the village. Upon inquiring about the source of the music, she was informed that it was coming from the nearby Mennonite Brethren Church. She was so fascinated by the sound of people singing that she pleaded with Mr. Wiens, her employer, to let her visit the church. It wasn't long before Helena was singing in the church choir.

In addition to singing in the choir and working for Mr. and Mrs. Wiens, Helena was able to assist from time-to-time with the chores at the Jacob Neufeld home. Even though she was still in her teens, her love and devotion for the Neufeld children apparently caught Jacob's eye. He was pleasantly surprised to see this bright, energetic, young girl work so diligently at the Wiens' home and also help with the housework and care for his family.

As time passed, friendship and admiration grew between Jacob and Helena. Despite the difference in age (he was forty-nine and she was nineteen), Jacob decided that he would approach Helena about becoming his wife. In her diary, during this time, Helena wrote, "I wanted to continue working and singing in the choir which I dearly loved. My immediate response was an absolute 'No,' especially since Jacob was so much older."

One of Helena's strong traits was her desire to be " . . . in the Lord's will," as her diary revealed. She began to pray about the situation, eventually telling God that if He wanted her to marry Jacob, she would obey "His will," and would give up her own desires, in spite of the wide disparity in their ages. She wrestled with the prospect night and day. She also considered the fact that because of Jacob's good reputation as a successful blacksmith and businessman, he would be able to offer a secure future. The fact that he was one of the leaders in the church was also appealing. Finally, she decided that she would consider marriage if Jacob could get approval from the minister and the church authorities.

It was unusual at that time for a man who had raised one family to be remarried, especially to a woman thirty years younger. Not only was there serious doubt in the minds of church authorities, but there existed the possibility that government officials might discover a legal basis to deny the relationship.

After several weeks of personal soul-searching and finally receiving the minister's blessing, Jacob and Helena were married on May 28, 1906, in Orenburg, South Russia.

Jacob heard that the blacksmith shop in Sparrau had been vacated by its owner. He decided to move back to Sparrau with his new bride and assume ownership of the same shop where he had learned the trade from his father.

He made arrangements to find homes for all of the children from his first marriage. Some had already married, others were old enough to marry and others found

Jacob Peter Neufeld, circa 1906

a livelihood working in people's homes, as was the custom of the time.

Jacob and Helena moved into an old house next door to the blacksmith shop. Helena was not pleased to live in the same old house where her husband was raised and she had thoughts of persuading Jacob to return to Orenburg. It was really the church and the choir that Helena missed. She had a strong soprano voice which she could demonstrate at a moment's notice. The church choir experience provided her with some of the happiest times of her life, as she wrote in her diary.

II

As Jacob and Helena attempted to establish a new home in Sparrau, outside forces began to impinge upon their plans and their livelihood. Various church members openly disapproved of Jacob's marriage and accused him of neglecting his children. It became difficult to attend church anywhere in the Molotschna Colony. The new couple was made to feel guilty and uncomfortable.

One day as Jacob was working on a wagon in his blacksmith shop, a government official rode up on horseback. He shouted, "Are you Jacob Neufeld?" Jacob laid down his forging iron and walked slowly toward the rider.

"Yes, I am Jacob Neufeld."

The rider threw out his arm toward Jacob and said, "Here, this notice is for you. You have one week to respond." He turned the horse around and rode off without further explanation.

Jacob opened the letter and read the notice carefully. He walked over to the workbench, sat down and read it again. He couldn't believe his eyes.

You are hereby informed that you have failed to pay government taxes in the amount of 450 rubles and you have failed to report your income status for the past year.

Furthermore, it has come to our attention that you are living illegally with a young girl.

It is necessary for you to respond to these charges within one week, or else you will be in danger of being arrested.

7

Jacob's chin dropped as he thought, *This is just another type of harassment that German settlers have to endure. There is absolutely no truth to any of this. This is exactly why so many families have moved away from here.*

It was also possible that Russian neighbors living in the Molotschna Colony had complained to the authorities and had accused Jacob and Helena of living out of wedlock. Jacob wasn't sure, but he and Helena began to pray seriously about it.

Several days later, Jacob and Helena were sitting at the kitchen table eating their noon-day meal when a horse pulling a sleigh came into the yard. The rider jumped off the sleigh and came toward the house. Jacob immediately went to the door, but when he saw the white-buttoned black shirt underneath the fur coat, he suspected the visitor was a government official.

Once again, Jacob was handed a written message. The visitor said, "You need to read the letter right now before I leave, because I will be back to pick you up."

The words of the visitor made Jacob so nervous and upset that he had trouble trying to open the envelope. Before he began to read, Jacob looked up at the man and said, "What do you mean, you're going to pick me up?"

The official, a coarse-looking man with long whiskers and a moustache, responded, "Never mind what I mean. I have been given orders to take you and the woman you live with to a different place. Read the letter and be ready in two weeks." He turned and strutted back to the sleigh, jumped on and drove off without a backward glance.

Jacob and Helena were devastated. They wondered how this could be happening to them. After all, hadn't they always worked hard to "serve the Lord" the best way they knew how? Why were they being punished when they were trying to live a peaceful life and provide goods and services for their friends and neighbors? Jacob always went the extra mile to help those in need, or extended the time for customers to pay back a debt.

They realized they didn't have much of a choice. Jacob informed his neighbors that he and Helena would have to leave and that the equipment and supplies in his shop were for sale.

He had worked hard to make sure his shop was stocked with leather and metal strips, timbers for building wagons, and wooden spokes with iron rims. He had prepared materials and equipment for the long, harsh winter when the weather would be too cold to work in the shop. His supplies were always in demand and his business had begun to flourish.

Within a few days he had sold nearly everything—everything except his two horses and a sturdy sleigh. Jacob had a plan. He heard that many German families had fled to Siberia and it was rumored that land there was free to new settlers.

He and Helena packed extra clothes and food in two large, cowhide bags. The neighbors seemed to grasp what was taking place, but they did not congregate in the Neufeld front yard. They did not want to be seen contributing to an escape. Some of them stopped by just long enough to say, "God be with you," and *"Aufwiedersehn."*

Jacob arranged for the sale of his property to Mr. Fast, who gave Jacob only a small down payment with a promise to pay the balance at a later date. Helena, who was an excellent seamstress, put the money into several cloth bags and sewed them carefully into selected places in her undergarments so they could not be easily detected.

Jacob made sure they had an extra set of warm fur coats, pants, caps and boots. Helena packed bags of biscuits and sausages and put them into one of the large bags. The time had come for them to leave.

As the horses strained forward to pull the sleigh, it made squeaking, crackling noises sliding over the ice and snow. It was a sad day as Jacob waved goodbye to his friends, his home and his blacksmith shop. Helena did not have the same warm feelings about Sparrau. She had better memories of her life in Orenburg and it was easier for her to give up the house and chores in Sparrau.

Helena had a new concern now because she was pregnant with her first child and had no idea where they were going or where they would be able to rest during the night. However, she felt quite secure with her husband, believing that he would be her provider and protector.

Because of her loyalty to Jacob and her faith in God, she was able to put most of her fears aside and muster the courage to make the journey.

Jacob thought about the children from his first marriage and wondered how they were doing. He realized that he might not ever see them again. It was difficult to accept what was happening. Running from the authorities and government officials was not something he ever imagined doing, and he wrestled with the thought of going back and turning himself over to the man who had said, "In two weeks I will be back to pick you up." However, he knew he had already made matters worse and that there was no turning back now.

As they distanced themselves from the little village of Sparrau, Jacob and Helena tried to imagine how long it might take to find other German settlers in a familiar environment. Jacob had no idea how far it was to Siberia. He hoped that his horses could pull the sleigh that far.

He stopped periodically to give the horses a rest and to stretch his legs. He and Helena took turns holding the reins so that the horses would not panic and start running too fast. When nightfall came, they stopped and gathered branches and dried-out bushes to build a small fire. They ate biscuits and sausages, consuming just enough to sustain them until they could get to a house or village—but they had no idea where or when that would be.

As they traveled further eastward, they noticed fewer and fewer trees. The terrain was becoming much more hilly and was more difficult to pass. The wind was steadily increasing and the chill factor made it miserable to ride on the sleigh. The horses were beginning to show signs of fatigue and their breathing was becoming more labored.

As the sleigh rounded the side of a tiny hill, they came upon a clearing that appeared to have been used as a trail. Far down in the valley below, Jacob thought he could see a glimmer of light. As he drove the horses in the direction of the light, he wondered what it could be. He thought out loud to Helena, "I wonder if there is anyone friendly in that place? It would be nice if we could go inside and get warm."

He continued thinking, *Or could this be a government outpost, and have the guards already received information about my flight from Sparrau?* Would he and Helena be subjected to abuse and be taken back to face the authorities on a trumped-up charge?

Helena spoke quietly, "I hope we can stop for a while for a rest and maybe share a fire." The ride was beginning to take its toll on her stamina. She could only last so long.

Many thoughts were racing through their heads, but they felt compelled to continue toward the light. When they got close enough to see better, a man appeared from inside the little shack and walked several steps toward the approaching sleigh. Jacob was straining his eyes as he searched for signs of friend or foe.

He stopped the sleigh, slowly got down and started to walk toward the man, always keeping a watchful eye on him, as well as the shack. Jacob almost slipped into his native tongue, German, but, fortunately, he caught himself just in the nick of time and spoke in Russian.

"Good afternoon, sir. We are trying to find the way to Siberia to meet our old friends and possibly settle down there." Jacob was hoping that the man, who was obviously a Russian guard, had not received information about the escape from Sparrau.

He thought he noticed a slight grin on the guard's face as Jacob continued to speak humbly, "My wife is with child and I was wondering if we could come inside just long enough to get warm?" He had seen some smoke coming out of the tin vent above the roof.

Finally, the Russian spoke. He pretended to be friendly. "Come in—come in. We have a small stove inside. There are just three of us."

Jacob helped Helena get down from the sleigh and walk up the steps into the little shack. The smell of liquor was so strong that Helena hesitated just for a moment, wondering what it was. Jacob asked himself, "What are these guards doing here? Why are they stationed so far away from any town or village? What is the purpose of their being located in this isolated spot?"

Jacob did not want to introduce himself and state his real name, which would reveal his nationality, and so he waited until he could hear the guard's name when his buddies called out to him.

As he looked around the room, Jacob saw rifles in a military gun rack and several boxes of ammunition on the floor. The heat from the stove began to penetrate through the thick layers of clothing Jacob and Helena were wearing. They began to feel a little more comfortable.

One of the guards, in the bedroom to the side, began to stir. He slipped on his boots and came to the door between the two rooms. "Who in the (expletive) have we got here, George?" He was huge with a grizzly-looking beard and a gruff voice.

George answered, "We have here a man and his pregnant wife who want to go to Siberia." Both men leaned over, slapped their knees, and roared with laughter. This awakened the third guard who decided he, too, wanted to see the "idiots" who dared to venture out here in this cold weather.

Jacob couldn't resist asking, "Tell me, why are you men stationed out here, so far away from any village or humanity?"

The huge drunk, standing in the doorway, answered Jacob's question. "We are here to shoot runaway fugitives, criminals, idiots, and men with pregnant wives." All three guards threw back their heads and guffawed heartily, which made Helena sick with fear. Where she came from, people didn't joke about such things.

Jacob wondered if the pot on the stove had anything in it. He struggled with the thought and decided to ask George, "Do you have something to eat in that pot?"

George said, "Sure, help yourself to the soup," knowing there was little left in the pot and that it was only watered-down broth.

Jacob walked over to the pot, picked up the ladle and brought the soup close to his mouth. It did not smell very good to Jacob, but he decided to take some in a small bowl to Helena. At least it was warm. They both took a few swallows of the broth and it felt soothing in their mouths and throats.

As Jacob sat on a stool pondering what the Russian guards might do to them if they tried to leave, he became fearful, remembering the drunken guard's caustic remarks.

Resting inside the outpost for about thirty minutes was all that Jacob could stand. He'd take a chance. He stood up, stretched his legs and arms, and announced, "Men, we are thankful to you for your generosity and hospitality, but it is time for us to go."

George gasped and blurted out, "You have to be crazy, man! There's nothing out there except hundreds and hundreds of miles of freezing cold weather. It's too far for horses and a sleigh to reach any village or humanity. We have taken many traitors out there to freeze to death. Think about it, man!"

Jacob knew that George was speaking the truth, but there was no thought of turning back. He was determined to keep on going.

As he and Helena thanked the men and began to walk down the steps of the shack, one of the guards was standing next to the horses and sleigh, as if he were inspecting the animals. Jacob took some money out of his pocket and gave it to George. He knew that the Russians would expect something in return for their kindness, but suddenly, he noticed the other guard by the sleigh, examining the contents of the two bags. He could see the exposed fringes of a blanket, a sheepskin jacket, and leather boots. Jacob thought, *Maybe I should give this guard some money and distract him from the clothes bag.*

Jacob did not realize that the drunken guard was not so interested in the clothes bag, but he really had his eyes on the horses. After the guard walked around the horses and the sleigh, he walked over to George and whispered something to him. Jacob suspected trouble and wondered whether he would have to fight the Russians if they tried to take his horses. He did not carry a pistol or a rifle because he and Helena did not believe in killing another human being, no matter what. But he was strong and physically able to take on two or three men in a fight.

He had been involved in several fights before in his life and had proved to be capable of defending himself. But his first thought was: Always try to settle differences or problems in a peaceful manner.

He took Helena by the hand and helped her up to her seat on the sleigh. As he started to climb aboard, the drunken guard, who had been admiring the horses, approached Jacob rather quickly. He spoke forcefully, "I will take you to your destination. I will drive the horses and when we get to your village, I will drop you off there and, in exchange, I will buy these horses and your sleigh. Don't worry, man, you will be well paid!"

Although he was suspicious of the guard's intentions, Jacob smiled and gestured, "I appreciate your offer, but I'm sure we will make it all right."

As Jacob climbed up to his seat, the drunken guard jumped on the lower front seat where the bags were tied, grabbed the reins, snapped them on the horses and yelled, "Giddup! Giddup!"

Jacob's mind was blurred for a few seconds before he realized that the guard was stealing the horses and the sleigh right out from under him. He began to think of all the horrible things that could happen to him and Helena.

They had to hang on tight because the guard was running the horses as fast as they could go.

Jacob thought about jumping on top of the guard and wrestling him off the sleigh, but that could cause the horses to panic and he didn't want to endanger Helena or the unborn child. As the guard lifted his arms, Jacob could see the pistol at his side under his coat. He could only think of holding on to the sleigh and protecting Helena.

The guard drove the horses for several hours without letting up, until Jacob thought they would drop. He noticed that the guard was allowing the sleigh to slip and slide sideways and in different directions. Jacob was anxiously trying to read the guard's mind. Was he thinking of causing a deliberate accident? Was he thinking of trying to dump them off?

They had come a long distance from the outpost and it was beginning to get dark. Jacob knew that the horses had to be rested, and he and Helena needed a rest break desperately. Suddenly, the guard turned the horses in a new direction and he snapped the reins on the horses over and over to make them go faster. It was as if the man knew precisely where he was going and was determined to get there in a hurry.

Helena began to panic. She looked out at the vast area of snow and ice, the lack of any visible evidence of humanity; no buildings, no shacks, no shelter of any kind. She also thought about how good God had been to her and how thankful she was for the wonderful things that had happened to her in the past. Was it all coming down to this? Were she and Jacob going to be left on this expanse of frozen wasteland to suffer and freeze to death? Helena was determined to control her emotions. She bowed her head and prayed devoutly—it was the only thing to do to avoid becoming hysterical.

The guard took the horses and sleigh down a sharp embankment and, at the bottom of the hill, they began to glide over a smoother surface. Jacob thought they must be on a frozen lake somewhere in Siberia. The darkness was making it difficult to tell where they were or in which direction they were going. Suddenly, the sleigh came to an abrupt stop. The horses' bodies were steaming wet with perspiration and they were breathing long streams of hot air from their nostrils. The guard decided to speak. "This will be a short rest stop so that you can stretch your legs."

Jacob thought, *Why didn't he stop when there were some small trees and bushes back there so that we could have a little privacy, especially for Helena?*

Jacob and Helena slowly stepped off the sleigh and tried to walk on the slippery surface far enough in the dark so they could not be seen. Suddenly, while they were whispering to each other about their plight, they heard the guard yell, "Giddup! Giddup!" The horses took off and the guard could be heard shrieking with laughter as he rode away with the sleigh and all of Jacob and Helena's belongings.

Jacob and Helena were stunned. They were alone in the bitter cold of the Siberian night. This was just like the many stories and rumors they had heard when they were living in Sparrau. They had heard how criminals, government dissidents and political prisoners had been banished to Siberia where they were summarily abandoned to freeze to death. It was not possible for anyone to escape this predetermined fate because the distance was so great and the bitter cold temperature would take its toll in a short time.

Jacob's first thought for survival was to walk far enough to reach land because he knew they could not survive even one night on the frozen ice. He took Helena by the hand, hesitating only long enough to pray out loud, "Oh God! We have always tried to be obedient to your word," and then he quoted Psalm 46:1, "God is our refuge and strength, a very present help in time of trouble."

Jacob knew the situation seemed hopeless, but he also was convinced that " . . . through faith in God, all things are possible." He touched Helena's cheek and comforted her by saying, "Everything will be all right, dear. God will take care of us."

They trudged along in almost total darkness for several hours. Helena's feet were beginning to hurt from the ice's sharp edges. Now and then just enough moonlight came through the clouds to allow them to detect a change on the horizon. Some indications of land were becoming visible, although completely covered with snow and ice. After stepping off the ice and onto what felt like land under the snow, Jacob knew that Helena had to rest. He didn't want her to sit or lie down in the snow, so he searched for a small embankment where he could place branches to cushion her body.

Finally, Helena was able to sit down and rest. Jacob took off his sheepskin coat and tucked it around her. He snuggled down as close to her as possible so that his body warmth might help her.

The temperature continued to drop. It was brutally cold, and the night seemed endless and frightening. Jacob thought about the possibility of frostbite and he knew that walking would help prevent, or at least delay, this. If only morning would come so that they could begin to walk again . . .

It was difficult to fall asleep, but they were so exhausted that they were able to get a few hours of much-needed rest. Frequently, they could feel themselves slowly sinking into the snow. As soon as the first glimmer of daylight appeared, Jacob urged Helena to stand and see if she could walk. He reached up to his face to break off the icicles which had formed on his eyebrows and his beard.

When he picked up his coat, he had to brush off several layers of new snow, but the warmth of the sheepskin garment was welcome. They began to trudge through the snow, having no conception of which direction to go. There was just a trace of sun behind the misty clouds. They tried to gain a sense of direction that would take them to the east, hopefully toward some evidence of humanity, or even better, to the area where there might be other German settlers.

They kept their eyes on the horizon which seemed so vast, so dismal, so utterly desolate. Miles and miles of snow loomed before them. As they continued to struggle through the icy, powdery stuff, Jacob stopped suddenly. Helena looked at him as if to ask why. He was focusing in a straight direction, and after hesitating for a moment, he said, "Helena, I think I see something—possibly a sled with dogs, but it's only a speck on the horizon."

They were apprehensive and anxious as they waited to see what the object might be. It was hard to distinguish. They had to wait until it came closer. Jacob could see something moving, but he didn't see a man. Was it a pack of dogs with an empty sled? If so, there would be no help coming. But wait! It appeared to be moving in their direction. Jacob bowed his head in a brief prayer and then looked up quickly. He lifted his hand to his forehead to shield his eyes from the blinding white snow. If there was a man, would he turn out to be friendly or another enemy? Maybe he wouldn't see Jacob and Helena and simply keep going on his way. What incredible emotions they were experiencing.

Jacob yelled and waved his arms. He wasn't sure they had been seen. To his great relief, a sled and dogs came into view and he thought he could see a person at the back of the sled. A person to be short in stature—but a real, live human being. Jacob yelled louder and waved his arms wildly; he couldn't jump up and down because of the soft snow, or he would have done this, too.

All of a sudden, the small man at the back of the sled waved. Jacob nearly passed out. His relief was overwhelming. The dogs appeared to be coming straight toward the couple. Jacob and Helena were not as afraid of the dogs as they were of the tiny man.

The dogs were barking so ferociously that for a minute Jacob was worried that they might get out of control and attack. As the dogs came closer, the two fugitives became terrified because of all the noise, but the small man yelled loudly and cracked his whip until the sleigh came to a full stop. Although the driver left his sled, he continued to hold on to the reins. It took him quite a while to quiet the dogs as he gave each of them something to eat.

He was a short man, whose eyes readily identified his Asian heritage. Jacob had heard of the Kirghiz people who were members of a Mongol tribe living in Siberia. The man turned toward Jacob and addressed him in a language Jacob had never heard before. Jacob tried to speak in Russian, but the Kirghiz man obviously did not understand. Soon both men were using their hands and arms to try to communicate. It didn't work. When Jacob and Helena referred to him, they simply called him "Kerrghee."

Kerrghee motioned to Jacob, pointing to Helena, who was unsteady and about to faint in the snow. He made a gesture with his arm to invite Helena to come and sit down on the sled. Jacob was apprehensive but he also felt the man showed signs of being trustworthy and there were no other choices available.

Helena was fearful but she needed the rest so badly that sitting down on the sled was a welcome thought. As she sat down, Kerrghee showed her how to strap herself in the sled. Then, he motioned to Jacob to walk on one side of the sled while he walked on the other.

Kerrghee led the dogs at a slow pace so that he and Jacob could keep up. Instinctively, Jacob knew it was going to be a long, arduous walk, but he was relieved that at least Helena was riding and could get some needed rest.

Knowing that he had to keep going enabled Jacob to find the determination and strength to stay with the sled. When Kerrghee stopped the sled to rest the dogs, Jacob gave a sigh of relief. He could rest his legs and see how Helena was doing.

After struggling through the snow for four or five hours, they saw a small cluster of buildings in the far-off distance. It was as if God had spared Jacob and Helena from a certain, freezing death, and now they would be inside a secure building, hopefully where they could relax and get warm.

The buildings turned out to be tiny shacks, placed in a circle around a larger shack, which was where the dogs and other animals were kept. Each shack had only one or two rooms. The larger shack in the center was the barn and this is where Kerrghee took Jacob and Helena.

Kerrghee said something like, "Follow me," as he motioned for them to come along. There was too much snow packed against the barn door, so Kerrghee took them around to a small door cut about ten feet above the bottom floor of the barn. He had to crawl through the small door, and climb down a ladder on the inside. He yelled to Jacob and Helena to follow.

It was easy for Kerrghee to get through the small door, but Jacob, with his much larger frame, had to squeeze against the sides of the entrance until he thought he would break the boards. Finally, he and Helena made it through the little door and down the ladder.

Once they were standing on the floor of the barn, Kerrghee pointed to one corner of the barn where Jacob and Helena could stay. There was a small room sectioned off by a wooden fence covered with animal hides. A few items, such as two small wooden stools and a small, wooden table were pushed to one corner. Someone else had used his "guest room" before. A small, pot-bellied stove stood in one corner and it didn't take Jacob very long to get a fire going. There were old places of hides and rags mixed with crushed bushes and stubble to keep the ground from being so hard and so cold.

Kerrghee bowed his head and disappeared through the crawl space to the outside. Jacob and Helena immediately dropped to their knees and thanked God for sparing their lives. So far it appeared that Kerrghee was a friendly man. Jacob wondered if he should ask for something to eat. They had not eaten since they tasted the soup in the Russian guards' shack.

When Helena took off her coat and boots, she sat down and began to rub her swollen and discolored feet to gain back some circulation. She was afraid that she might have damaged her feet so badly that she wouldn't be able to walk. Jacob came over to look at her feet and helped her to rub them gently as their bodies began to thaw out by the stove.

Jacob decided to look around. He could hear animal sounds coming from the other side of the barn but he couldn't see them. A tall wooden structure separated him from the other side. Once in awhile dogs could be heard growling and snarling at each other. *That's it*, he thought. *The dogs have to have something to eat!* Maybe Kerrghee would feed them and remember to bring Jacob and Helena something to eat also . . .

As it began to turn dark, they heard some creaking noises. The tiny barn door opened and in came Kerrghee and a female companion, presumably his wife. The woman carried a pot of tea in one hand and two cups in the other. Kerrghee placed a small pot of stew on the table. Jacob and Helena were overcome with emotion at this act of kindness and hospitality.

Helena could not contain herself. She stood up on her sore feet and gave Kerrghee's wife a big hug, which can be understood in any language or nationality. Helena had tears in her eyes as she told the woman in German, "Thank you, dear lady, thank you, dear friend. You have saved our lives and now we have something to eat. Thank you, thank you, thank you."

Kerrghee and his wife smiled, bowed their heads, turned and exited through the crawl space, while Jacob and Helena were attempting to thank their benefactors in German as well as in Russian.

The hot tea tasted strange to Helena, but at least it was warm and good, not only to swallow but to feel the cup with her hands. Jacob started to smell the stew and quickly backed away.

He looked at Helena and asked, "What kind of animal do you think they slaughtered to make this concoction?" The unfamiliar smell caused him to be suspicious.

Helena placed the ladle in the broth, brought up a small amount, smelled it, and gently put her lips to the ladle. She took a small amount of broth into her mouth, tasting it carefully. "Jacob, it has some unusual spices in it. That is why it smells so strange to you."

After tasting the broth several times herself, Helena finally convinced Jacob to try some of it. He became more accustomed to the unfamiliar taste and was just thankful to have something warm to eat. Kerrghee's generosity was truly appreciated as the couple ate most of the stew. As they prepared a place on the floor for a night's rest, Jacob reassured Helena, "Don't worry, everything will be all right. God has brought us this far and He won't abandon us now."

As they lay inside Kerrghee's barn, somewhere in Western Siberia, they both cried and thanked God for protection and for sending Kerrghee to save their lives that day. They had been taken all the way from a horrible, freezing death to a comfortable, warm place in Kerrghee's barn. If George and the drunken guards could see them now!

III

Early in the morning, as the pale winter sun began to rise, Kerrghee went about the business of feeding his animals. When the dogs heard him coming they began to bark wildly, because they knew food was on the way and they were ravenous. Kerrghee threw each of them a piece of meat which they pounced on and devoured within seconds. Jacob had checked the barn and discovered other animals: three cows, four pigs and two horses. The horses' protruding ribs revealed a sad lack of nutrition, and the other animals looked very lean.

While checking over the contents of the barn, Jacob noticed an old, broken sleigh and two sleds. If he could convince Kerrghee that the sleigh and sleds were reparable, and that he had the expertise to do this kind of work, he might be able to repay Kerrghee for his kindness. The problem was communication. Kerrghee spoke neither Russian nor German, although every now and then he would mention a town or village which had a Russian name. Jacob listened intently each time these places were mentioned.

As he tried to communicate with Kerrghee, Jacob repeatedly engaged him in conversation. "What are you going to do with that old sleigh in your barn?" Jacob asked. "Would you like me to repair it for you?" They looked at each other in frustration as each tried to understand unfamiliar sounds. There was much yelling and gesturing. Jacob would repeatedly point to objects and then say the word that matched the object, trying Russian first, then German, but Kerrghee could only smile and shrug his shoulders.

Finally, Jacob decided to begin working on the old sleigh and the sleds, while keeping an eye on Kerrghee's reaction. Gaining confidence, Jacob slowly began to cut strips of animal hides, using them to tie sturdy branches together. As Kerrghee watched Jacob reinforce the sides of the sleds, he began to show signs of excitement, suddenly realizing that he was going to be able to use the old sleds again.

After Jacob repaired the sleds, he pointed toward the sleigh. Kerrghee responded by gleefully shaking his head up and down. He quickly ran to the old sleigh and pulled it into a clearing so that Jacob could work on it. It didn't take Jacob very long to strengthen the glides attached to the body of the sleigh. He had repaired many sleighs back in Sparrau. His blacksmith skills enabled him to rebuild this one entirely. Not only did Jacob repair the sleigh, but he also reinforced the harnesses and all of the straps required to pull it.

That evening Kerrghee and his wife brought two baskets of food and another pot of stew into the barn for Jacob and Helena. Even though they couldn't communicate very well, Jacob knew that Kerrghee was showing his appreciation for the work done for him.

After a meal of white rice and cooked fish, Jacob spoke softly to Helena. "Today I heard Kerrghee repeat certain words which lead me to believe that there may be a village to the east of us where there are people who look and speak as we do."

He continued, "They are either Swedish or German—I can't tell for sure. I think I heard the names of two places where we may need to go to find this village. It sounded like Kerrghee said 'Omsk' and 'Pavlodar,' two large cities in central Siberia."

Helena listened intently as Jacob spoke. He continued, "If we could get to one of those towns, I'm sure we could find the village—and maybe other German people like us. Let's pray and ask God to touch the heart of this friendly Kirghiz man, so that when I ask him tomorrow to take us in his sleigh, he will be willing to do it."

The next day Jacob had an idea. He tried again to communicate with Kerrghee. He spoke to him in Russian and mentioned the sleigh, all the while gesturing and pointing. He went into the barn and brought out the sleigh. Then he called for Helena to come outside and stand next to him. He pointed first to Helena, then to himself, and said, "Omsk, Pavlodar," "Omsk, Pavlodar," over and over again, all the while pointing in the direction he thought would be correct.

Finally, something clicked. Kerrghee smiled and moved his head up and down. Jacob was so pleased that he extended his hand for a handshake, but Kerrghee didn't understand the gesture.

Helena went into the barn and began cleaning up their "room." The cups and utensils were returned to Kerrghee's wife and Helena began packing the few things that had not been commandeered by the drunken guard. She made sure the cloth bags of money were still securely attached to her undergarments.

While Jacob was outside helping Kerrghee hitch the horses to the sleigh, he couldn't help noticing again how thin they were. Even though they had been given food and water that morning, Jacob was concerned about their health.

As Jacob and Helena climbed on the sleigh, they

were pleasantly surprised to see Kerrghee's wife coming toward them with a small package. Inside were dried strips of meat, several small biscuits, and two pieces of fish that had been cleaned and fried. Food enough to last for about two days. Helena was overcome with emotion as she thanked this generous woman over and over in Russian and in German.

Kerrghee's wife patted Helena's arm, and her smile said that she understood. Helena would never forget that smile and the kindness extended to them by the Kirghiz couple. In fact, as she looked at the tiny woman, so different from herself in every way, she thought, *This must be an angel sent to us from God.*

Kerrghee jumped on the sleigh, took the reins, and urged the horses forward to parts unknown. Jacob and Helena waved to Kerrghee's wife repeatedly until she was out of sight. Then Jacob began wondering: did Kerrghee really know where he was going?—but he had to trust him.

The sleigh seemed to veer over unusually rough terrain as the ice and snow cracked beneath the weight of the three passengers. Helena was five months pregnant now and was fearful that the rough ride might harm her in some way. She thought that it was probably a good thing that the horses could not go at top speed. The slower pace helped make the ride a little smoother for her.

After crossing over several miles of rough terrain, and nearly tipping over when the sleigh hit a hidden rock, Kerrghee suddenly let out a howl and pointed in an easterly direction. Jacob and Helena's eyes strained forward as they tried to see something. As they came closer and closer to an object on the horizon, they realized that it was a village. When they got to within a hundred yards of the first house, Kerrghee called for the horses to stop and he motioned for Jacob and Helena to get off the sleigh. He made sure they had the bag of food that his wife had given them, and then he reached over to pick up one of his extra coats, which he handed to Jacob.

The men just stood there and looked at each other. With great emotion, and throwing caution to the wind, Jacob threw his arms around Kerrghee and gave him a big bear hug. "Thank you for all your kindness! You not only saved our lives, but now you have brought us to this village. God bless you and your wife. We will never forget you."

Although slightly startled, Kerrghee seemed to understand. However, he was definitely not interested in staying there too long. Jacob realized that Kerrghee was probably afraid to come into the village for fear of being kidnapped by the villagers and held hostage against his will.

As soon as Jacob and Helena got off the sleigh, Kerrghee snapped the reins and the horses began to pull the sleigh which, mercifully, was much lighter now. Jacob and Helena had tears in their eyes as they waved goodbye to the man who had saved their lives and displayed a true friendship. As they watched Kerrghee go, they waved until they could not see him anymore.

Turning toward the village, the couple looked at the first house. Who were these people and what problems would they present? When they were approximately fifty feet from the first house, the front door opened and out came a man and two women, followed by several children. Jacob decided to speak in Russian first: "We have traveled a long distance and are very tired. Would there be a place in this village where we could stay for a brief rest?"

Jacob was apprehensive about revealing his true heritage, but as the adults began to speak and introduce themselves, the man from the house said smilingly, *"Ich bin Johann Isaacs,"* in the most beautiful German Jacob had ever heard. Jacob's grin stretched from ear to ear as he answered, *"Ich bin Jacob Neufeld, von Sparrau, South Russia."*

They grabbed each other's hands and the ladies began to hug each other. Jacob and Helena could not hide their tears of joy. They were alive and with friends! Quickly they were ushered into the house, where they were offered fresh bread and hot coffee, a warm fire and a comfortable room.

The Isaacs were German Mennonites who exemplified a humble way of life. They were dressed in plain, black clothes; Johann wore a wool shirt, trousers, and boots that laced halfway to his knees.

Frieda, Johann's wife, wore a long, dark-colored wool dress that buttoned tightly around the neck and wrists. Whenever they stepped out of the house, they threw on sheepskin coats to protect themselves from the cold.

The Isaacs' house was a simple, three-room structure, but the rooms were large enough to provide living quarters for more than one family. The smell of pine and the smoke coming from the pot-bellied stove combined into an irresistible aroma that made Jacob and Helena quickly feel at home. They thought they had never smelled anything so delightful.

As Jacob chewed a piece of the delicious brown bread and slurped the hot, black brew, he had so many questions that he couldn't talk fast enough. "Tell me, Johann, where is this place? What kind of people live here? Do you own this land? Is there more land available here?"

Johann smiled, "Wait a minute, Jacob. One question at a time. We have twenty-two German families living here in Revrovka, and yes, there are Mennonites who live next door to those who are not German. Sometimes, a Russian family will move into the neighborhood. In regard to the land, there are many acres available, if you are willing to work hard and take the risk. As you know, the Siberian winters are very harsh. You will be interested to know that we are approximately one hundred miles from Omsk, the largest city in central Siberia."

Jacob thought of Kerrghee when Johann mentioned the city of Omsk. Jacob began to feel that this might be the right place to live. As he was deep in thought, he realized that Johann was grinning. "Jacob," he said, "it's time for you to take a warm bath and put on some clean clothes."

Frieda was making her pregnant guest welcome also. She made preparations for Helena to have a warm bath and gave her fresh, clean clothes. Helena thought nothing had ever felt so good. However, she kept a vigilant eye on her undergarments where the money was sewn. She rolled these into a small package, which she hid in the bedroom.

When Jacob and Helena retired for the night, they both knelt beside the bed to give God their sincere thanks. They were in a new part of the world, but, mercifully, in a place where they could easily communicate with others. Jacob still had many questions for Johann.

After enjoying a hearty breakfast of hot coffee, bread, eggs and sausage, Johann took Jacob for a ride through the village. Johann had beautiful horses and a sturdy sleigh. He told Jacob that he knew most of the families who were living in Revrovka—the Jantzens, the Friesens, the Goertzens, the Hieberts, and the Unruhs. There were others, and Jacob would come to know them all.

Johann explained, "Jacob, the government is giving free land to new settlers and you could qualify for as much as one hundred acres and free seed for planting."

Jacob could hardly wait to see the land and sign the contract. He answered Johann with an exuberant, "I want to start right away!" The winter snow and ice would soon melt and the ground would need to be prepared for planting.

As they rode through the village, Jacob kept looking at the ground. He knew it would only be a short time before planting season.

Johann pointed out the school, a one-room building where teachers from the village volunteered their time. There was another tall building where the grain was stored, and Jacob got to see the old-fashioned threshing machine.

Johann explained to Jacob, "One out of every six barrels of grain has to be returned to the government at a warehouse in Omsk. The rest can be stored for family use or sold to neighbors who can afford it."

They passed by several houses and Johann stopped the horses in front of one of them. He said, "Jacob, come inside and see if this vacant house would be suitable for you and Helena."

At first Jacob was a little apprehensive because the house looked rather small, but he quickly remembered that God had protected him and Helena and brought them safely here to Revrovka. Surely they would be able to live in this house. "Yes, of course," he said, "this will be quite suitable. We need to settle down, especially now that Helena is about to give birth to our first child."

That evening Jacob had many nice things to tell his wife. As they talked, they both became more and more excited about their new house, and the prospect of having their own land to farm. Suddenly Jacob thought of what was missing. He blurted out, "The blacksmith shop!" *Where was the blacksmith shop?*

The next morning Jacob sought out Johann and asked him whether there was a blacksmith shop in Revrovka.

Johann couldn't believe his ears. "You mean to say that you are a blacksmith? That is exactly what we need in Revrovka," he exclaimed. "We always have to travel long distances to get our wagons repaired and to shoe our horses. Oh, Jacob, you will be the talk of the village! You will be in great demand here. The people in our village will be absolutely thrilled to hear that we now have a blacksmith."

As he listened, Jacob thought he was hearing an angel. It was settled. He would have a new home and he would build a blacksmith shop right next to the house.

Shortly after they moved into their new home, Helena gave birth to their first child, a beautiful baby girl whom they named Marie, after Helena's mother, Maria. Jacob had used some of the money which Helena had hidden in her clothing, to buy needed items for the house, such as a table and chairs, a wood stove, a bed and blankets. Many items were donated by kind neighbors, but Jacob was able to pay for furniture by repairing wagons and harnesses. His services were in great demand and it didn't take long before he had enough money to make a down payment on lumber to build the new blacksmith shop.

The next few years passed smoothly for Jacob and Helena. They began to raise a family, which made it necessary for Jacob to add several rooms to their house. He built a large barn for his animals and a shop to house the equipment and supplies needed for his blacksmith trade. Within a relatively short time he had acquired horses, wagons, sleighs, harnesses, metal and leather straps, and wooden wheels with metal strap binding. He was prepared to conduct business, and he wanted to help his neighbors. He gradually became a productive member of the little village of Revrovka.

The land proved to be unusually fertile and soon Jacob and Helena had the satisfaction of seeing many acres of beautiful grain.

As the couple reflected on everything that had transpired over the past few months and years, they had no way of knowing that their future would hold unbelievable hardships beyond their imagination.

IV

On September 7, 1908, Helena gave birth to the couple's first son. He was named Jacob, in honor of his father. However, their joy was short-lived; little Jacob became ill and passed away during the winter of 1909.

The death of the baby boy, attributed by his mother to pneumonia or diphtheria, was extremely difficult for Jacob to accept. If it had not been for the strong support of other German families and his strong faith in God, Jacob would have experienced a severe depression. Many families brought food and gifts to the Neufeld home, as was the custom. A small memorial service was conducted in the house because there was no church building in the village.

The people were anxious to have a church, but rumors about the treatment of Germans in Russia caused the elders of the "church" to use caution in building a new place of worship. They knew that in many other areas inside Russia, German people were being persecuted. Anti-German sentiment exploded during the 1870s when Russian peasants realized that the original plan—that of having Germans move to Russia to teach the Russians how to farm—had gone awry.

Most of the German emigrants were religious and cultural separatists. They were successful at raising grain and cultivating the land, but they tended to isolate themselves from the Russians and any outside influences. The Russians interpreted their isolationism as elitist and after many years of trial-and-error, anti-German movements began to spring up in the Ukraine and other areas inside Russia.

While Jacob and Helena were busy raising a family, building a successful blacksmith trade and increasing their grain production, they heard of other German families escaping from the Ukraine and emigrating to Siberia, to Germany, the United States, Canada, and South America. They heard how anti-German sentiment had influenced the government to look the other way as roving gangs of hoodlums and robbers invaded village after village. As these gangs spread throughout the country, they killed the men and children, raped the women, and remained in each village only long enough to eat whatever food was available.

Leaving the Ukraine in 1907 turned out to be a stroke of luck, or as Jacob would say, "The hand of God." The couple felt secure in their new home, but they were greatly saddened to hear the horror stories about the land from which they escaped.

Things were going well for Jacob and Helena and they soon welcomed a second baby boy into their family on April 1, 1910. They decided to name him Jacob because the first Jacob had passed away.

Cornelius, or "Corney," was born on October 18, 1911, followed by John on May 10, 1913, with Henry joining the family on September 18, 1914. Then, surprise, surprise, they hit the jackpot! On April 22, 1916, another beautiful baby girl! Jacob insisted that she be named after her mother and so they settled on "Helen."

Marie soon found that she was growing up in a family where the work never ended. She had to help her mother take care of all the boys and her little sister. Because of so many chores, Marie had little time for school, or for that matter, anything else. She was constantly kept busy changing diapers, bathing the latest baby and helping Helena in the kitchen. She was happy to have a sister and she hoped that Helen would grow up quickly and be able to help around the house.

At this time, Russia was beginning to be consumed with chaos and political unrest. The Communists took over the government in 1917; Jacob and Helena heard it said that Lenin had pronounced those terrible words, "We will conquer the whole world without God." These atheistic comments struck great fear into the hearts of the German people in Russia.

Soon it became impossible to meet in large groups for church services. Each family had no choice but to arrange for Bible study and worship services in its own home. Sometimes it was possible to conduct quiet services with several families present.

When Joseph Stalin came into power, the anti-church (or anti-Christian) movement became much stronger. Premier Stalin decreed that anyone found reading the Bible, praying, or attending a church service could be put to death.

The people in Revrovka were anxious and fearful as they read about the persecution of Christians. Johann and Frieda Isaacs had received correspondence from their relatives in Russia and paid a visit to Jacob and Helena to share their news.

"Just read this letter from my sister and look at these pictures," said Johann. The letter described in detail what was shown in two photographs.

Jacob read how an entire congregation of believers had been forced to evacuate a church. Jacob turned to Helena and said, "This photograph shows the people lined up outside the church, about sixty-five men, women and children—and look, Helena, the minister is hanging from the church steeple!"

Jacob and Helena sat in stunned silence as they stared at the second photograph, which showed all of the people from the church lying supine in the snow after having been shot and killed. It was unthinkable, but true. They looked at each other and immediately embraced, unable to speak, tears streaming down their faces.

Johann and Frieda came closer and put their arms around the sorrowing couple. As they wept together, Jacob managed to repeat the words of Job, "Though He slay me, yet will I trust Him."

Joseph Stalin was determined to wipe out all forms of Christianity and religion, even if this meant putting to death millions of innocent people.

As the new government came into power, and at a time when the country was being besieged by German armies from the West, the Union of Soviet Socialist Republics (U.S.S.R.) was in dire need of food and supplies for its army. The people in Revrovka were beginning to notice strangers riding through their village. It was not easy to determine who they were because they were so heavily dressed for the cold weather. The men in the village would try to meet at one another's homes in order to determine what was going on. They agreed that all families should be warned to be careful, particularly when visiting the larger city of Omsk. They knew they must guard their conversations and must always speak in Russian, not German.

When Jacob carried grain to the government warehouse, he began to notice that Red Army officials were always present. They were watching everything very closely. On one of his routine trips to the warehouse, Jacob was told that from now on he must bring twice as much grain. Of course this meant twice as many round trips on roads which were treacherous with snow and ice.

At about this same time, the village received terrible news. A rider had gone through the little town of Revrovka and ordered all families to bring their horses to a designated location. It was already evening but Jacob had no choice. He had to take his two best horses to a place about seventy-five miles away, and it had to be done immediately. When he returned home, Jacob told Helena the sad details. In his brief autobiography he wrote, "I led the horses, one on each side, while I walked in the middle. Two men came up to me, and before I knew what was happening, each one took a horse, jumped up on its back and rode away. I stood there in shock, not knowing what to say or think."

He decided to hang around the area for awhile, thinking an official might give him some money for the horses. Eventually, a soldier told him that if he had the proper identification, he could go to the office and get payment. Jacob presented all of the necessary papers for identification, but he was given only 100 rubles for each horse.

By the time he got back home to Revrovka, he was told the rubles were practically worthless. When he went to the local storehouse, he discovered that the money would be just enough to pay for a dozen boxes of matches. This—for his two beautiful horses.

The next pronouncement to the little village was that everyone was to keep enough grain, seed and bread for their family, but all of the rest was to be given to the government. Being completely honest, Jacob measured exactly what the family would need of flour and food, and he delivered the rest to the warehouse. As he finished taking the last load and was on his way home, Jacob was told that he had to go to the meeting house and hear the next public announcement.

When he arrived, two Red Army officers were explaining in crude, but no uncertain terms, what was expected of each family in Revrovka. One of the officers looked at Jacob and said in a stern voice, "Identify yourself!"

Jacob answered, "My name is Jacob P. Neufeld." The officer looked over a list which he held in his hand. He looked at Jacob and stated arrogantly, "We are going to divide your land into four parts. That way more people can share in land ownership and everyone will be better off. Now we want you to take all of the seed you have saved for the total acreage to the government warehouse."

Jacob later wrote in his diary, "The officer was a very young man, seventeen years old at most. He stood before me with a cocked gun, and in a loud voice ordered me to drive the grain to the station early in the morning. He stood there waiting for my answer. Then he yelled, 'What do you say? Make up your mind or I'll make it up for you.' Without realizing what I was saying, I answered, 'Yes, I will do it.'"

Jacob was on the road for at least three weeks. In order to keep from freezing, he walked most of the time, and as a result, became ill with a severe cold. However, before going to bed that night, he loaded the sled with sacks of grain. "Otherwise," he wrote, "the officers would have shot me dead."

When the soldiers found out that Jacob was ill, they forced one of the neighbors to take his horses and sled to the warehouse. It took the neighbor three days to make the trip. After that incident, Jacob was forced to make more trips, even though he still had not recovered from his illness.

One night, after arriving back at his home at about 11:00 P.M., he was getting ready for bed when suddenly there was a sharp knock on the window. "Open up, quick! It is a search!" came a warning from the outside. Jacob wondered why they would want to search his house, as if he had robbed someone. As soon as he opened the door, six men barged into the room. The first two held Jacob, one hand on each arm. The others began searching the house, looking for anything that could be used by the Red Army.

The soldiers opened every container and drawer in the house looking for grain, flour, potatoes, beans, lard and meat. They took whatever they wished, loading it on the sled outside. They picked up coats and boots and threw them on the sled also.

After taking everything of value from the house, they went into the barn where they found saddles and harnesses, and loaded them on the same sled. This looting went on for several hours, until there was nothing left. Jacob was forced to stand by the door in his night clothes and bare feet while he watched the men ransack his house. A lot of snow had been dragged into the house through the open door.

As Jacob stood there, helpless and unable to resist, he wondered how the children were doing. He could tell that Helena was trying her best to keep the children quiet and comforted. Little Jake, now fifteen years old, kept his eyes pinched shut and pretended to be sound asleep as the soldiers scurried around, opening and slamming doors and drawers.

At one point, Helena realized that Jacob was standing by the open door, with nothing to keep him warm.

She grabbed an old shawl, walked into the front room and threw the shawl to him. One of the soldiers screamed at her, "If you don't want to be shot like a dog, you better get out of sight!"

Finally, the men released Jacob and told him that he must deliver the loaded sled immediately. He was to take the load to a courthouse in a Russian town about fifty miles away. There he would receive further instructions. Helena tried to give him a warm bite to eat but he was instructed to hurry. He drove off with what appeared to be nearly all of the family's possessions: clothes, food, blankets and supplies.

By the time Jacob left the yard, an officer was there to make sure that everything they had loaded was still on the sled. He stayed with Jacob for the entire trip. As they rode along, he decided to engage Jacob in casual conversation.

He spoke up. "The new government is going to be good for all of us. Everyone is going to cooperate and help each other, don't you think?"

Jacob knew that to disagree with the young man would be dangerous and so he responded, "I hope so," but he couldn't help wondering just how much this rider really knew about the new government.

When they arrived at their destination, the sled was unloaded by placing everything on a huge pile of other supplies, right on the snow. Then Jacob was ordered to go inside an unfamiliar building. Immediately he recognized one of the men who had been at his house and had taken his belongings.

The man, dressed in military uniform, approached Jacob and said, "You are so healthy and strong, and you have beautiful horses and wagons. And that property you have is pretty good land, isn't it? How much can you earn with all of this stuff? I bet it's plenty. From now on, we expect you to bring it to us—your grain and anything else we need. If you give it freely, we will take care of you so that you will not have to suffer. But if you are difficult and obstinate about it and hold out on us, then woe unto you! We'll wipe you and your family off the face of the earth."

Another soldier walked over to Jacob and stood directly in front of him with a loaded gun. He shouted at the top of his voice into Jacob's face, "Tell us, are you going to bring us more grain?!"

Jacob tried to explain that he had only enough grain for food and that he had no seed grain for the next year—that he couldn't possibly bring any more grain unless someone helped him. The soldier crowded against Jacob and cursed him, put his hands on Jacob's chest and pushed him against the wall. The soldier yelled, "Yes or no! Not a minute longer!"

Jacob, being overwhelmed with fatigue and fear, answered, "I will, I will. Just don't hurt me. Please, don't shoot me; please don't shoot me!" Finally, they shoved him toward the door, showed him again to the outside, and yelled a stern warning to bring the grain immediately.

As he drove the horses homeward, Jacob began to agonize. What now? Would he have to *buy* grain to deliver to the government? His storage bins were empty and the money he might receive was nearly useless. When he arrived back at the village, he and a few neighbors got together and worked out a plan. Jacob would deliver a load for each neighbor and they would share with him so that every third load would be credited to him.

When he entered his house, Helena and the children were standing in a circle around the wood stove, weeping, praying and trying to stay warm. They were literally shaking and trembling in great fear. They had been robbed at gunpoint and their father was in grave danger. The terror in his children's eyes caused Jacob to feel sick to his stomach.

Helena did not want to make things worse by asking a lot of questions, but the children could not resist. "Where have you been, Pa?" little Jake asked. "We've been waiting for you and Mama has been so worried."

Jacob shrugged his shoulders and said, "I'm sorry, but I have been very busy hauling supplies for the government. But I don't want you to worry about it. I am able to take care of myself and you will be all right." He attempted to dispel their fears.

As Jacob continued to haul grain to the government warehouse, it was becoming apparent that many disabled soldiers were being discharged and were returning from military duty. As a result, Jacob was told that he had to transport the returning soldiers from Omsk to Pavlodar. The village government headquarters would pay him for this and he agreed to perform the assignment in order to get money to buy grain seed.

When spring arrived and it was time to plant, Jacob sought out the head of their town government, a Russian official, to inquire where he might find seed. "You go find your own seed," the official barked. "By the way, you're Jacob Neufeld, aren't you?"

"Yes, I am, sir," Jacob replied.

The official had a big grin on his face as he handed Jacob a written note. Jacob began to read: "You are hereby ordered to bring all of your blacksmith shop equipment, itemized list attached, to the government warehouse at Omsk. These materials are needed for the Red Army immediately."

His face dropped and his heart sank. He was now faced with losing his last vestige of a livelihood. He returned home, his heart filled with grief and sadness. He began to think about his family and how hard Helena worked to make clothes for the children. By this time the family had grown to include seven boys and two girls. In addition to her other duties, Helena had to spin the wool and sew every garment the children wore.

Baby Frank was born on November 27, 1918, just one year after the Bolshevik Revolution. His brother, Bill, was born on May 7, 1921, followed by Dave, born on December 17, 1922. Throughout these years, Jacob was desperately trying to meet the demands of the soldiers by hauling grain and supplies to the warehouses.

As he began to take his blacksmith equipment out of the barn and place it on the sled, Jacob was overcome with discouragement. When would all of this end? How could he support his growing family if he had no equipment in his shop and no seed to plant?

After delivering the equipment to the warehouse, Jacob was told he could make some money by transporting eleven Red Army inductees to Pavlodar. He was willing to take the risk in order to earn money. He needed to buy grain seed so desperately that he accepted this dangerous assignment. It took eight days to haul the men and their gear to Pavlodar, through difficult terrain and terrible, muddy roads.

In order to fulfill an order from the government, Jacob sold three horses, two cows and eighteen sheep, which gave him enough money to buy grain seed. But the family had no flour or bread and no warm clothes for the severe Siberian winter ahead. Jacob knew that the only clothes the children had were those Helena had made and which they were wearing.

It seemed that the more Jacob tried to satisfy the authorities, the more demands they placed on him. He always owed them something. When he got close to paying them off, they would add more to their list of requisitions.

In the spring there was nothing to sow, and in the fall there was nothing to harvest. An entry in his diary at that time tells it all: "I was always afraid that during the night something frightening would happen. Most of the demands came during the night, and then they were always so urgent. Hardly a night passed that there wasn't some kind of an emergency or disturbance. I was so discouraged and bitter that my family and I decided to leave our home in Revrovka and relocate somewhere else. More than anything, we would prefer to get as far away from Russia as possible, maybe to America."

Jacob knew that moving away from Revrovka would be very difficult, if not impossible. How would he manage to take his wife and all their children to a new location when he had no money? Where could they go where they would not be oppressed?

V

Even though Jacob dreamed of going to America, he had heard little about the United States. Jacob was eight years old when Abraham Lincoln was assassinated—but he had never heard of Lincoln. Theodore Roosevelt was President of the United States when Jacob married Helena, but again, he knew nothing about this president either.

It was 1925 and all Jacob knew about America was that his brothers, Abraham and Peter, were there. They had escaped from Russia and were living with their families in a land of freedom and peace. He knew this to be true from tidbits of news coming from the German Mennonite newsletter, *Zionsbote,* which circulated information about other Mennonites in Russia and in churches and communities in America.

He missed his brothers. In fact, more than once he told Helena that even though he was happy that Abraham and Peter were safe in their new country, thinking about them being so far away brought tears to his eyes.

Jacob knew that conditions were bound to get worse. The time had come. He must move his family away from Revrovka. He thought that somewhere to the east, where other Mennonites had moved, would be safer for them. Once again, they would have to make a fresh start.

A visiting family from another village in Western Siberia was traveling east and had stopped at the Balzer home in Revrovka. The Heinrichs family was on its way, hoping to reach the Amur River Valley. Mr. Heinrichs was accompanied by his wife and four children, and by his brother, William Heinrichs, whose entire family had been left for dead by Communist soldiers.

Jacob and several other men decided to pay a visit to the Balzer home where the Heinrichs family was staying. They wanted to hear more about this unbelievable tragedy. In the days before CNN and the nightly news, this was the way information traveled.

William was reluctant to repeat the story, especially with women and children present, and so they asked all of the children to go into the bedroom. The mothers quietly withdrew to the bedroom also, taking the children with them.

When the men were alone, they pulled their chairs close to Mr. Heinrichs. It was difficult for him even to begin. He was bent over and tears streamed down his face. The pain in his voice prevented him from speaking above a whisper.

He began: "One evening, as my wife and two daughters sat down in the living room after finishing the dishes, there was a loud knock at the door. Before I could stand up to answer, the door flew open and four soldiers rushed in with their rifles and bayonets.

"One of them said something about me being a filthy, rich farmer. I knew right away they had mistaken me for a John Heinrichs, who had accumulated a large acreage and many farm implements, and was known in our community as being well off. That man lived on the opposite side of our village. The soldiers were mistaken, but as I began to explain to them who I was, one of them struck me across my neck and shoulder with his rifle. I fell to my knees. Excruciating pain came from my ear down across my chest."

Mr. Heinrichs hesitated. Seconds grew to minutes. Jacob realized the old man was having so much difficulty speaking, that he looked like he was going to faint. Moving his chair closer to Mr. Heinrichs, Jacob put his arm around the man's shoulder and urged him to go on.

"As I fell, one of the soldiers said, 'Good, now just stay there on your knees and pray to your God.' Then they ordered my wife and daughters into the bedroom where they were told to undress. There was a great deal of noise and scuffling taking place in the room as the girls cried out in terror. One of the soldiers then made me walk on my knees into the bedroom where I was forced to watch as they raped my wife and daughters.

"I cried out loud, 'Oh, God! Please save us!' And before I could say the last word, I was struck on the side of my face with a rifle barrel. I was stunned, dizzy with pain. But I had to watch as they shot each one of my loved ones and shoved their bodies toward me on the floor. Then they forced me to walk on my knees through their blood.

"Suddenly, they pointed their rifles at me. I cried, 'Please, no. Please, no.' Then they shot me six times and one soldier slammed his bayonet into my chest. I lay there, knowing my life was over. The men ran out of the house thinking they had killed us all. But, through some miracle and the will of God, I lived through the terror. I can't understand why God spared my life when my dear wife and daughters had to suffer and die in such a cruel way.

"Now I am deformed. The pain is constant. However, I thank God for sparing my life and allowing me to come along with my brother's family to visit you."

Words of condolence failed to come to Jacob. The other men were speechless. How could human beings be so cruel? Moved by Mr. Heinrichs' story, they fell to their knees, thanking God for sparing this man's life and making it possible for him to tell what had happened. Before leaving that day, all of the men agreed that they must move. Their families were not safe. It had now become urgent.

Having heard that the Trans-Siberian Railroad was being completed, Jacob went to Omsk to talk to the ticket master about the possibility of buying a ticket for his family to travel by train further east, perhaps as far as the Amur River Valley. He explained that he wanted to go where there was good land to cultivate.

The ticket master spoke harshly: "Who do you think you are? The trains are full of soldiers and government supplies and you have the nerve to ask for a ticket!"

Jacob thanked the man for his trouble and decided to stand at a distance to see if others were able to buy tickets. He noticed that a man walked up to the ticket master and slipped him a few rubles. The ticket master whispered something into his ear and the man got into a different line. In the second line, when he reached the station attendant, Jacob could see the man take a roll of bills from his pocket and squeeze it into the attendant's hand. Immediately the attendant's attitude changed. He began to smile and treat the man with respect. They spoke in a friendly and polite manner.

So this was the way that he had to do it. Grease the ticket master's palm! Jacob did not like the idea but if that was the only way, then that's what he would have to do. But it would have to wait for another day. He had to get back to Helena and the children.

When he arrived at home he found that not all was well. He learned that Jake, Corney and Marie had decided on their own to go to Omsk to look for work. They were old enough to do this and certainly needed the money. Helena gave them food for their journey and prayed with them before they left.

About a week went by when Jake and Corney returned home without Marie. Jacob and Helena were irate. Jacob asked, "How could you do this?"

The boys explained that Marie had decided to go to work in the home of a Russian family. After all, they rationalized, she was twenty and capable of taking care of herself.

But Jacob and Helena were uneasy with the idea of Marie being out there somewhere, alone in the world. This was not what they had in mind. The entire family began to pray that Marie would be safe. Her sister, Helen, cried, "Marie just has to come home, Papa! She has to come home."

One morning, government inspectors came to Jacob's barn and began looking at his pigs. As Jacob went outside to greet them, one of the men yelled, "How much grain did you feed them?"

Jacob answered, "These pigs haven't received one handful of grain." The two inspectors withdrew to confer with each other. When they returned, they brought with them several young men and asked if they thought the pigs had been given grain. The young men began to laugh and swear, saying it was impossible for pigs to look that good without feeding them grain.

The inspectors turned toward Jacob and yelled, "Traitor! You are against our government. You are ordered to deliver these pigs to the government center immediately and wait there for further instructions!"

Jacob's hands trembled as he reluctantly told Jake and Corney to load the five pigs into the wagon and deliver them to the center. He knew that with the present political climate, anyone called a traitor or accused of anti-government actions, could be put in prison or sent to forced labor on roads or railroads. However, Jacob's prayers must have been answered once again, because several days went by and nothing happened. The inspectors had apparently forgotten about him.

He still had two horses, but Jacob was having a terrible time earning enough money for food. The family had little clothing because the Red Army soldiers had confiscated their warm garments every year for a number of years.

With each passing day, there was only one thing on Jacob's mind. They had to get out of this place and move to the Amur River Valley.

Jacob and Helena had traveled a tremendous distance twenty years before when they moved from Sparrau to Revrovka, some 2000 miles. Now, the family was large. Another move would be incredibly difficult. Jacob had no maps and he didn't realize the distance to the Amur region. Later he would learn that it was about three thousand miles!

As he struggled to earn enough money for food and clothing, Jacob was becoming more and more concerned for his family. He made numerous trips to Omsk to apply for permission to move, but each time he was rebuffed or required to complete the necessary paperwork, only to be turned down again.

On one of these trips to Omsk, he heard a rumor that the need to send government supplies and equipment on the train had been filled and that tickets to points east might be available. After submitting reams of paperwork, at last, Jacob received permission. His family would move to the Amur Valley.

Jacob knew that government officials didn't really care much about people traveling eastward in Siberia. They considered the entire region to be such a desolate, bitter-cold, forsaken land that the people would probably starve or freeze to death anyway.

Jacob was pleased as he made the return trip to his home in Revrovka with train tickets in his pocket. He and Helena lost no time in making arrangements with their neighbors to take whatever furniture there was in the house and to distribute anything extra. Jacob teasingly told some of his friends they owed him ten rubles, and others fifty to one hundred rubles. But it was only in jest. As he affectionately slapped his friend, Johann, on the back, he said, "You can pay me back the next time we meet!" knowing full well they might not ever see each other again.

Luck seemed to be with Jacob. His daughter, Marie, decided to leave her job as a housemaid and returned home to Revrovka. She arrived just as Helena and the children were preparing for the move, intensifying the excitement in the air. They all looked forward to a new land and another new beginning. There wasn't much to pack because they had been reduced to only the clothes they were wearing. There were a few extra pairs of boots and caps, but certainly not enough warm coats and blankets.

Their faithful friend and neighbor, Johann, offered to bring Jacob and the family to Omsk. They would ride on Jacob's wagons, which would become Johann's property after the Neufeld family boarded the train. Johann had harnessed his own horses to pull the Neufeld wagon so that Jacob's horses could follow behind. These were tied to the back of the wagon, along with one cow. With tearful eyes, Jacob and Helena loaded the wagon with as many supplies as possible, and then told their sons and daughters to climb on. The youngest son, Herman, was still a tiny baby and had to be held by Marie, his big sister.

"The time has come, we must go now," Jacob told them.

Jacob wiped a tear from his eye and whispered to Helena, "We enjoyed many good years in Revrovka and if the government had left us alone, this would have been a wonderful place to live." As they began to move, they waved goodbye to their friends and neighbors who represented a significant part of their lives for some twenty years. Jacob wondered how long they would be safe.

Turning their faces forward toward an uncertain future, each was lost in his own thoughts, knowing that once again they would have to rely on the will of God.

The weather was still cold from the winter snows, but there was a hint of spring in the air, making the trip tolerable. After all, there was really no such thing as a warm and cozy day in Siberia. It was always cold, so they knew they had to dress accordingly.

After traveling for two days and nights through melting snow and thick mud, they arrived at the train station, where they unloaded their sacks and belongings on the snow. Helena had one sack of food which contained sausages and biscuits. She kept this sack close to her, afraid to let it out of her sight. Johann stayed with them until the train arrived, so that Jacob's horses could remain tied to his wagon.

The children were reminded by Helena, "Go behind the station and take care of your personal needs before you get on the train."

As they waited, other German families arrived. Jacob felt better knowing there would be others on the train with whom he could associate, and they could face the journey and hardships together.

He had paid a high price for passenger train tickets and for space in the cattle car for two horses and a cow. But when the train was nearly loaded, Jacob was told there would be room in the cattle car only.

"Take it or leave it," the guard said.

They crowded into the cattle car together with several other families, and at this point, they knew there was no purpose in complaining. Nothing was going to improve and there was no turning back.

The cattle car was covered on top, but the sides consisted of boards approximately four inches apart. When they started moving, the wind rushed right through, creating a chill to the bone.

As the train began to move, each family had to snuggle together to try to stay warm. There were no restroom facilities on the cattle car and some of the children soon began to cry. It was embarrassing to "go to the bathroom" right in front of so many people. Several of the men decided to tie cow hides together in one corner of the car to make a relatively private place for this purpose.

The train did not travel very fast and the young boys tried to pass the time by peering out of one side of the car to watch the scenery go by. Mile after mile of snow with small pine trees dotting the hillsides certainly did nothing to hold any young boy's attention.

Jacob's sons began to have ambivalent thoughts. Where in the world were they really going? Was it really a wise decision to go further into Siberia? Maybe they would have been better off in Revrovka. The boys voiced their concerns out loud and asked their father many questions, but each time he reassured them that they were in God's hands. "He will take care of us," Jacob said.

As the train chugged along uphill, it would slow down to five or ten miles an hour, sometimes barely moving. But when it went downhill, it picked up plenty of speed. Each day the train made several stops, allowing the passengers to disembark, get some exercise and use the opportunity as a "restroom" stop.

The bitter cold of the trip, the fact that people were crowded so closely together, and no running water or sanitary facilities available caused many to become ill. Some had severe sore throats and fevers, and others developed terrible coughing spells. Before the trainload of miserable passengers had reached its destination, several had died.

The boys' faces showed discouragement that even Jacob's "pep talks" could not cure. Once in awhile their interest was revived when the train passed over a bridge and they could see a raging river in the gorge below. But the tedious trip made tempers short.

Helena's sack of food had grown alarmingly slim. She was forced to give each child less to eat each day. No one had anticipated that the trip would take so long. It would have been impossible for Helena to have packed enough food for so many mouths for such a journey.

After twenty-one days on the train, people began to stir and talk expectantly to one another. It was as if they sensed something. Some acted as if they could see something in the distance. Jake and Corney leaned against the outside boards of the railroad car and squinted against the bright snow to see what the commotion was about. They heard some of the men saying that they could see a town far off on the horizon. They thought it might be Blagoveshensk, a city known to a few of the travelers.

The boys repeated the difficult name over and over until they could pronounce it correctly.

Jacob was sure in his mind that Blagoveshensk was the right town, their destination. As they came closer to the lights of the city, people on the train began moving around.

As the train slowly approached the outskirts of the town, the eager passengers could hardly believe their eyes. The sign at the station clearly read Belogorsk. Jake and Corney climbed over the side of the cattle car, jumped to the ground and ran ahead to the station. They soon came running back to tell everyone that this was not Blagoveshensk, and that they would have to transfer to a side track which would take them to Blagoveshensk, a distance of about one hundred and twenty miles.

Although there had been deaths and sickness, and children were hungry and thirsty, there now seemed to be a new spirit in the air, a little excitement about finally being so close to their "real" destination.

The train came to a halt and people began to unwind their stiffened limbs. They had now been in the cattle car for twenty-two days. What an exuberant feeling to be able to jump to the ground!

Helena and Marie kept the younger children in one group as Jacob and the older boys took the two horses and the cow off the cattle car. Jacob was pleasantly surprised to learn that there were about twenty other German families on the train. They began to pass the word along that there would be a group meeting. At this meeting it was decided that the families would stay together as the men looked for horses and wagons to move everyone to the Amur Valley.

The group stayed in Blagoveshensk for several days, long enough for each family to get its horses and wagon, and enough food and supplies to last for the final leg of the trip. This part of the journey would take them over a mountainous terrain for about one hundred and twenty miles and into an area near Poyarkovo, near the Amur River. It would take nearly a month to travel from Omsk to this final destination.

At long last they arrived and gazed at their new surroundings. Jacob bowed his head, then said to Helena and the children, "There seems to be a lot of open land here and the soil looks rich and fertile. Maybe this is where the Lord wants us to live. Let us pray and be thankful."

One of the more pleasant surprises was that the Russian officials of the district seemed to be more cordial than those encountered in the past. Each family was given about forty acres for farming and there was ample pasture in the hills for the livestock. It was time to start all over again. A new village was born.

VI

Jacob was surprised and his sons were impressed. There were large steamships traveling back and forth on the Amur River. Even though they didn't know what was on them, the family began to feel rejuvenated about the new possibilities in this region. The other families in the village became enthusiastic about the land and the future.

The older Neufeld sons, Jake, Corney and John, took on the responsibility of plowing the land. It was May, 1928, when Jacob began to build a small house for his family. His plan was to build a larger house in the future and then use the smaller one for grain storage.

Their plow and seed grain were borrowed from the government and Jacob's two horses were used to till the ground. All of the German families worked their farms together, helping each other with the planting of seed.

As soon as the small house was completed, Jacob collected materials to build a larger one. He made hundreds of bricks to be used in building their new home. Helena and Marie planted a large garden in which they grew red and green cabbage, carrots, onions and potatoes. Jacob wrote in his diary, "It is a pleasure to watch the garden grow so beautiful, particularly because Helena and Marie have worked so hard preparing the soil and planting the seeds."

For the first time in many years, things seemed to be coming together for the Neufelds. But, their peace of mind was short-lived, however, because news came to them from neighbors that the Amur River was beginning to rise dangerously. It was the summer of 1928, and the ice and snow were melting fast. The Amur extended far north and west into the Manchurian Mountains and it became a huge waterway as it followed its course to the Sea of Okhotsk.

The weather took an ominous turn for the worse. It began to rain harder than anyone had ever seen before. The wind whipped the rain horizontally against the sides of the house and showed no sign of letting up. Jacob stated with grim humor, "If it doesn't stop soon, I'll have to build an ark."

The situation soon became serious as the deluge continued day and night for several weeks. It seemed as though some gigantic heavenly faucet was turned on with the water pouring directly over their heads.

The rain, together with melting ice and snow, caused the Amur to rise to the top of its banks. Jacob heard reports that the tributaries coming from the north and west were already flooding. Traveling was out of the question. Their village was now isolated and in grave danger.

Government airplanes flew over the area dropping leaflets warning the settlers to move to higher ground immediately because when the river crested, the flood water would be higher than their homes.

Jacob and the older boys quickly put some lumber and hay on the wagon and rode to the nearest hill. They selected a spot and hurriedly put together boards and rafters, which they covered with hay so that they would have some shelter to crawl under.

In the evening they rode back to the house where they found the rest of the family in great fear. Panic was everywhere as the people rushed to seek higher ground. Jacob and his neighbors spent the entire night going back and forth trying to rescue their belongings.

Jake and Corney were sent to the river's bank to determine how high the water level was. Jacob instructed them to stay on high ground, but to get as close as possible to the river. He wanted their first-hand account as to how dangerous the situation really was.

The boys came running back shouting, "It's just about to flow over the bank, Papa, we need to run for our lives!"

Jacob yelled, "Everyone! Up the hill!"

The four oldest boys picked up their rowboat and carried it as fast as they could. Other families were doing the same thing. It was a scene of mass confusion as the adults shouted orders, each trying to direct their own family. Older children carried crying babies and the smaller children struggled to keep up with the others.

It was almost impossible to keep their footing because of the pouring rain, which had turned the ground into a sea of mud. Children cried out in fear as they repeatedly slipped and fell. Everyone was soaked to the skin.

As they scrambled up the hill, occasionally the boys had to stop and rest. Somehow, that rowboat got much heavier the longer they carried it. Jacob and Helena stayed behind the children, making sure everyone was accounted for. Frank, Bill and Dave took turns with Marie and Helena carrying little Abe and baby Herman, who was only one year old at the time.

As they struggled up the hill with their few possessions and the rowboat, darkness settled in. Finally, they reached a place where they thought they would be safe.

The younger children were completely exhausted and crawled into the rowboat where they quickly fell asleep.

Jake and Corney tried to remain alert, keeping their eyes and ears open for warning signs from other families, in case someone sounded an alarm. Some people huddled together in groups, trying to comfort each other. Many were fervently praying.

Helena passed out biscuits to the family, which they ate in a state of utter exhaustion. After this meager "meal," each one found a place to lie down to get some rest.

The four older boys, Jake, Corney, John and Henry, could not sleep and were too worried to lie down for long. Corney spoke to the other three, "Do you think we are high enough to be safe from the water?" He was a strong brother but also prone to being overly concerned. This time he had good reason to worry.

John was a little more relaxed and calm as he suggested to Corney, "Let's just make sure everyone else is all right. We can take turns watching and try to get some rest."

The night dragged on. There was no moon and the rain continued. Suddenly, at 2:00 A.M., there was a thunderous explosion. Immediately following this terrifying noise, the roaring sound of water came crashing through the village where they had been just hours before. They were frozen with fear. It seemed like the whole earth was being engulfed in water. Trees, pieces of wood, parts of houses and furniture all mixed with water and mud were moving through the valley. The terrifying sounds were amplified in the darkness. This created such panic that some of the people became hysterical.

Water seemed to swallow the hill where the Neufeld family had been sleeping. The boys yelled, "Get in the boat, get in the boat—hurry!"

They barely had time to get everyone inside the tiny craft. Jake and Corney stood at each end of the boat, waiting for the water to arrive. As the first wave splashed against them, the boys managed to move the boat along with the force of the water, carefully holding on and jumping in at the last minute. The boat was now free from land and they were at the mercy of the water.

As they tried to account for everyone in the darkness, they yelled each other's names and were reassured that all were present. The little boat tossed about in many directions, sometimes tilting dangerously to one side and then the other.

After being carried downstream for what seemed an eternity, a gleam of daylight began to appear—a welcome sight! Things began to take on a whole new dimension. They realized they were far from their original destination and perhaps a mile or two off shore. Helena was holding Herman, Marie was holding Abe and the rest were just holding on to each other, hoping the boat would not capsize or be broadsided by some large piece of floating wood. Tree trunks were rushing by like so many match sticks.

Jake and Corney tried to find the oars, but they were hidden somewhere beneath all that humanity. After searching and getting everyone to move a little, they found first one oar and then the other. They began to row toward shore.

The distraught family became a little less fearful as they approached land. Corney jumped out of the boat first and grabbed the bow to drag it to shore. Slowly, one by one, they climbed out of the tiny craft that had saved their lives.

After pulling the boat onto shore, the boys went up a little farther to look around. They waved back to the family to follow them. When they gathered at an open spot on the welcome land, Jacob and Helena immediately fell to their knees to thank God for saving their lives once again.

With overwhelming emotion, Jacob said, "We have gone through many terrible experiences and have had close brushes with death, but never anything like this."

Their physical and emotional fatigue was so great after the past hours and days that they dropped to the ground right where they were standing and fell asleep.

After a short rest, the family began to survey the desolate scene. As they gazed upon what looked like a watery, muddy grave, they realized their home, furniture, personal belongings—all their possessions, were buried somewhere under that sea of mud and debris. Everything was under water and their possessions were out of sight.

Obviously, many other villages had been destroyed along with their own. No one knew how many people had lost their lives, but the thought caused Jacob to shudder. The Neufelds didn't know which way to turn. There was no path or road to travel on—no physical landmarks, trees, or vantage points to use as a guide. They had no food, water, or extra clothing. Their only hope was to start walking toward higher ground and keep looking for shelter and people who might help them.

As they climbed higher, another problem presented itself. Huge numbers of mosquitos, ants, gophers, snakes and rodents of all kinds had been forced out of their underground homes. The rain had flooded the burrows and the animals were at war with each other, each one frantically seeking to find food and defend itself. Rats and mice reacted viciously, attacking each other and anything else that got in their way.

Not only was it difficult and painful to walk under such conditions, but mental despair began to take its toll. Some of the boys tried to beat off the attacking animals, but the younger boys were literally frightened to tears. Herman and Abe were carried, but most of the others had to walk, and as a result, suffered painful bites.

Jacob determined that there could be no stopping, even for rest, until they could escape from these animals. They continued to walk along in single file, with Jacob in the lead and with Jake and Corney in the back. There was nothing in sight that resembled human habitation.

Finally, after struggling for two days and nights, completely exhausted and thinking they could go no further, the older boys pointed to a house, just outside a small village. They walked in the direction of this house, but Jacob had them all stand still while he studied its appearance, wondering if anyone inside would be friendly.

He didn't want to walk into a trap, with the possibility of getting into a scuffle or being hurt. He continued to watch the house carefully and waited to see if anyone would come outside.

Since there appeared to be little activity at the house, he gathered his courage and walked to the front door and knocked.

After a few moments, which seemed like an eternity, the door opened revealing a woman with several children behind her. She spoke in Russian and Jacob began to explain his predicament: "Please, dear lady, I have a wife and eleven children outside—all of them very tired and some are sick. We haven't had anything to eat for days. Could we please come in to rest, and if you have anything to eat, I would be happy to work for food. I would be most grateful—please, it is a matter of life or death."

The woman looked at Jacob, then glanced past him at the children, then stared intently at Helena. Still, she hesitated to give a response. People in this part of the country were always fearful of strangers because they had heard of families being robbed and killed by roving gangs of hoodlums. She started to close the door, but as she did so, she looked at the children again. They were a pathetic sight, with their clothes torn, their bodies full of sores and bruises, and covered with mud. They were certainly no band of robbers.

It was obvious that the lady of the house realized this family had escaped from the flood and was now completely destitute. Her face became compassionate and she beckoned Jacob to come in. They introduced themselves and found out that the lady's name was Anna, and she had three children living with her.

The Neufeld children entered the house and most of them sat down on the floor and immediately fell asleep.

Anna and her children had little to offer, but she said, "I will cook some potatoes and cabbage from the garden."

Helena offered to help her and, as they worked together, the room began to fill with the most wonderful fragrance: food. It was an aroma which caused the children's empty stomachs to growl.

Each child was given a bowl of vegetable soup and for the older children, as well as for Jacob and Helena, Anna made hot tea. Jacob couldn't thank Anna enough. After they had eaten, most of them fell asleep again right on the hard, wooden floor. It was the first time in many days that they were not hungry and now they felt safe and warm.

Anna listened intently as Jacob and Helena explained their desperate situation. She agreed to let the family remain in her home until they could find some assistance elsewhere. As far as the Neufelds were concerned, Anna must surely be an angel.

The next day Jacob headed toward the village to look for help. He wanted to find someone in charge. He was directed by strangers on the road to seek out an individual who called himself the mayor. When he finally found the mayor, Jacob explained to him, "My family lost all their possessions in the flood and my wife and children have escaped to your village with nothing."

The self-appointed mayor, a large Russian with a booming voice, detected that Jacob was of German descent, and he reacted very coldly to him: "Go into the village and beg for something to eat. Somebody might throw you a slice of bread."

Jacob was obviously disappointed when he heard the man's response. He could sense a deep-seated resentment toward German people. The more he tried to reason with the mayor, the more upset Jacob became. There were other Germans in the village by now and native Russians were blaming many of the local problems on them.

Jacob left the office of the mayor and began to walk slowly down the road. He had no idea what he would do or where he would go. Maybe he could find assistance of some kind at another place where someone would listen to him and give him advice. As he trudged along the road, discouragement overcame him. He was hungry, lonely and depressed.

Suddenly, as if appearing out of nowhere, his oldest son, Jake, yelled, "Pa! Pa! I have everything ready. I found the office where they help the needy and the survivors from the flood!"

Jacob couldn't believe his eyes or his ears. Jake was supposed to be at Anna's house helping Helena care for the children, but he had decided that Jacob might need help, and after all, there were plenty of brothers and sisters who could babysit.

Jacob rolled his eyes toward heaven and said, "Thank you, Lord. And thank you, Jake." Jake told his father that the official he met was making plans to give orders to the townspeople. They had heard about the flood and people were being urged to help those in need.

Jake had a written order in his hand which could be traded in for enough flour and bread to last for a month. Also, if anyone in town had jobs or work that needed to be done, they were to hire those who had escaped the flood, or at least, give them first chance.

A week later, Jake, who was eighteen, was able to get a job assisting a land surveyor. It was the money from this job which enabled the family to subsist for several months.

Jacob was astonished at the way God had spared his family. Now he would be able to go to the mill with Jake to get a sack of flour. However, when they arrived at the mill, Jacob began to realize that he couldn't possibly carry a sack of flour all of the way to Anna's house. There was no transportation in that direction and the road was too muddy.

After thinking about their problem, the mill clerk offered his horse. He told Jacob, "Put the sack on the horse's back and when you get to your destination, remove the sack, turn the horse loose, and he will find his way back to the mill."

Jacob shook his head in amazement and thanked the man profusely. What surprise gift would he receive next from the Lord?

Anna, Helena and their families anxiously waited for Jacob and Jake to return. When they arrived with a sack of flour, it seemed like a holiday.

With Anna's permission, Helena took the flour and baked *schnetkia* (biscuits) for everyone. Not a crumb was wasted. When they finished eating, Anna thanked Helena and said, "I have not seen bread for a long time; it tastes so wonderful."

Everyone went to sleep that night grateful for full stomachs, thankful again for Anna's hospitality, for God's protection, for the horse that carried the sack of flour, and even for the hard floor on which they slept.

Working for the land surveyor, Jake earned forty rubles a month plus food and lodging. Jacob and several of the other sons found enough work cleaning yards and picking up trash to earn a little money. After about a month, they had enough to rent an old weatherbeaten house which had to be patched with mud to keep out the wind.

Jacob and Helena thanked Anna by leaving her with a good supply of baked bread and biscuits. She had done so much for the Neufeld family, allowing them to stay so long at her house. During the time there, the children, who had arrived with many insect and rodent bites, had become healed and much stronger.

Winter was approaching and the "new" house was wet and cold. There was no wood to patch the cracks in the house and very little for a fire in the stove. The walls inside glistened with ice. With no warm clothes, no blankets or bedding, the little house felt like a freezer box.

The government had promised disaster relief for those who had lost everything in the flood, and while Jacob got his hopes up, no assistance ever came. The Communist government officials were placing heavy demands on the people, who were expected to turn over the bulk of their food and grain. Anyone who opposed them was immediately put in jail, no warning or explanation.

The free flour was stopped. The mills were taken over by the government, and flour could not be purchased by anyone.

However, Jake and Corney found a secret way to buy a sack of flour at night time from a downtown location and sneak it into the house. If they had been caught, they would have been treated as traitors to the Communist government and jailed immediately.

Life for the Neufeld family became precarious as winter arrived. Temperatures fell to thirty and forty degrees below zero. The children shivered uncontrollably from the bitter cold and their mother had but little warm food for their stomachs.

To make matters worse, Jake's income was taken away from the family when the Red Army drafted him into their service. Jacob and Helena became emotionally overwhelmed when this happened. They had escaped the hardships of the Ukraine, the persecution by Red Army soldiers in Revrovka, the terrible, devastating flood, and now they were to contend with the unbearable thought of Jake being drafted. This was an intolerable situation for them. It violated their allegiance to God and the very core of their beliefs.

VII

Jacob sat up night after night. He knew that it was decision time. He and Helena had nine boys and two girls to think about. Herman was the youngest, nearly two years old; Abe was three; Dave was six; Bill was eight; Frank was ten; Helen was thirteen; Henry was fourteen; John was sixteen; Corney was seventeen; Jake was eighteen; and Marie was twenty-one.

Jacob and his family would have to try to escape from Siberia. But how would they manage to take all these children and attempt to cross a frozen river into China? Their lives were hanging in the balance. Yes, they might be captured and even killed trying to escape, but if they stayed, "Surely, we will starve or freeze to death," Jacob told Helena.

So many desperate thoughts weighed on Jacob's mind. Marie had found a job as a house maid, working for the Klassen family. He knew approximately where the Klassens lived, but he didn't want to take the risk of visiting their home in order to get Marie. The Klassens lived north of the Amur River, about ten miles away.

As Jacob sat in the chilly sod house, he munched on a small piece of "Rugga brot" (a dark-grained wheat bread), and pondered on how to get word to Marie. He was afraid to step outside because Red Army guards seemed to be around every corner throughout the neighborhood. He knew they would relish questioning him, discovering that he was German, and possibly placing him under arrest.

71

In addition to his family problems, Jacob was also becoming weak because of his hunger and cold. He worried about his son, Jake, who had been inducted into the Red Army. Just when he needed a strong son to help them escape, Jake was miles from them and would not hear about his father's plans to escape from Siberia.

The situation began to affect the entire family. Helena, Corney and John tried to assure each other and the younger children that everything would be all right, comforting each other with a smile and a warm embrace.

Winter was settling in now and some of the children found it hard to breathe. The temperature was reaching 20 to 30 degrees below zero, and even though they were inside the hut, their lips were blue and their teeth chattering. There was nothing to be cheerful about and the prospects of finding food or even the hope of finding warmth were dwindling.

Jacob and Helena were, once again, at wits' end. Would God provide a way out this time? How many times could they expect Him to spare their lives, and how could there possibly be a solution to their present dilemma?

Jacob knew that there were other German families in the neighboring vicinity and he had heard that a few families had made it across the frozen Amur River into China.

He spoke to his sons, Corney and John: "I want you to walk to the bank of the river and see if there are Red Army guards patrolling. Do not say or do anything to attract attention to yourselves. Act as if you are just taking a leisurely walk to see the river."

Henry heard what Jacob was saying and immediately spoke up, "But Pa, Frank and I were just down there yesterday and we know . . . "

"Shh, Henry," Jacob interrupted. "I want Corney and John to go now to see today how many guards there are and how often they pass by."

Turning to Corney, Jacob cautioned him, "Now, you need to try to be very inconspicuous. Mind your own business. I need to know the exact conditions of the river bank and how it is being guarded. Go now, and be very careful!"

Jacob needed to find horses and a wagon, but he had only a few rubles in his pocket. He dared to walk out of the house and hurriedly walk down the road. Fortunately, he met an old man, a Cossack, who had two horses he wanted to sell. He was afraid the government would confiscate his property, so he willingly agreed to deal.

With scarcely enough money in his pocket, Jacob also negotiated for a wagon and harnesses. While acquiring the animals and the wagon, he came into contact with several other German families who had moved into the area so that, when the time was right, they could also make their escape to China.

Everyone Jacob met agreed that each family would be on its own once the escape was attempted.

Like the other groups, Jacob loaded the children and supplies on the wagon, making every attempt to reduce the total weight to prevent cracking the ice.

The plan was to have two men leading the horses, one on the left side and one on the right, to hold on to the bridle and control the animals. This would also help to calm the horses and keep them from panicking in the event of loud noises or if the wagons should break down.

Most of the families were large, with grown children, and so older boys volunteered to walk alongside the horses.

As the dangerous venture was played over and over in their minds, the family tried to think of every possible situation that could arise because they knew there would be serious and even fatal consequences if anything went wrong. If they were caught by the border patrol trying to flee from Russia into China, they would all surely die. However, they were determined to try because they felt there was no choice.

Corney and John had scouted the escape area. They reported to Jacob that they saw the patrols, Red Army guards on horseback, passing back and forth along the river bank. Usually, at noon, the guards would meet at a place where they ate lunch and relaxed for awhile.

Jacob knew it would be dangerous to make the attempt at night because of the darkness. Trying to find the right clearing from the top of the river bank down to the ice would be nearly impossible. There were many small bushes and trees growing on the bank but an opening would have to be found.

Jacob and Helena found themselves, again, bracing for the worst, while praying for God's protection and guidance. Once again, Jacob repeated Psalm 46:1; "God is our refuge and strength, a very present help in time of trouble."

He must have repeated it a dozen times, occasionally changing to Psalm 23:4; "Yea, though I walk through the valley of the shadow of death, I will fear no evil, for thou art with me, thy rod and thy staff they comfort me."

On March 29, 1929, Jacob received an unusual surprise. Someone was coming toward the house. He was wearing a Red Army uniform and seemed to be in a big hurry. In an instant Jacob recognized the soldier. It was Jake, his oldest son.

"Jake, Jake, it's so good to see you!" Jacob ran toward his son, wrapped him in an embrace and cried for joy.

Jake was so tired he could barely speak. He blurted out, "Pa, I sneaked out of camp several days ago and ran nearly all the way. Has anyone been here to ask for me? I'm surprised they haven't caught up with me by now."

"No, but you better get in the house, quick, and take off those clothes," warned Jacob. "We'll have to think fast about what we are going to do. We can't stay here any longer."

Helena and the rest of the family were overjoyed to see Jake. They had reluctantly accepted the tormenting thought that they might never see him again. While he was changing clothes, Jacob spoke privately to Helena: "We must quickly prepare to make our escape; if the military authorities find Jake, he will certainly be put to death. If only Marie were here, then we could all leave together."

Jacob was going to contact several other German families about his plan to escape, but he had to act in secret and there was not enough time to reach them all.

On March 30, 1929, Jacob and Helena decided it was time to go, even though Marie was not with them. They could not chance staying in their house any longer, even though the attempt to escape placed all of their lives in jeopardy.

At high noon, with the temperature below zero, Jacob and Helena put the children, nine boys and one girl, on the wagon, along with a few clothes and a small bag of food. They traveled slowly to the river bank trying not to arouse any suspicion.

As Jacob drove the horses up to the top of the bank, he noticed a well-traveled trail along the river bank. This was the trail that the soldiers used to patrol the river, passing each other in opposite directions every half hour to one hour.

Since it was now noon-time, Jacob thought maybe the guards were inside eating their lunch. As the family moved along the river bank, trying to find a suitable place to go down to the ice, Corney spotted a patrol guard coming around the bend. He quietly whispered to Jacob and Jacob thought, *Oh, oh, this is it. We will be caught, arrested, and maybe killed.*

Jacob pulled on the reins and stopped the horses. Everyone sat in silence and waited for the inevitable. The patrol guard came straight toward them. The children's eyes were fixed on the guard and Jacob was ready to be friendly with a smile and a greeting. As the guard came closer, he did not even slow down or appear to be interested. He simply waved and kept on going.

Jacob's heart was pounding and the rest held their breaths. Jacob noticed that the guard couldn't have been more than sixteen or seventeen years old, and possibly in a hurry to meet one of his buddies for lunch. Jacob wanted to make sure that it wasn't a trick and he whispered to the family to remain still until the guard was completely out of sight.

Then Jacob nodded to Jake and Corney to continue down the path in order to find a suitable place to go down the side of the river bank. When they spotted a clearing to the ice, Jacob told everyone to hold on tight as he turned the horses downward, off the trail, and into the brush below. Jake and Corney held on to the horses' bridles, but they couldn't hold the horses back as the weight of the wagon pushed them down the slippery slope. The boys and the horses were helpless to slow things down. As they came crashing down the slope, the boys lost control of the horses and fell away from them to the side. The horses, wagon, family and all crashed downward through bushes and undergrowth, but fortunately missed several trees.

Everyone on the wagon bounced around and bumped into each other as the wagon came to a stop in an upright position at the edge of the ice. Jake, Corney and John quickly inspected the harnesses and the bottom side of the wagon. They waved to Jacob that everything seemed to be all right. They would now begin the treacherous journey on the ice.

At this location, the Amur River was almost two miles wide. It was frozen solid but very uneven, with many sharp peaks and ridges, as if the waves and swirling currents of water had been frozen, suspended in motion.

The thickness of the ice was unknown and could be extremely deceptive. It could have been three to five feet deep or thin as paper and might crack without warning. It was going to be a frightful experience before they would reach the other side, to the land of China. To freedom.

Jake and Corney held on to the horses' bridles and slowly moved forward. The horses seemed to sense that they were being compelled to do what was almost impossible. As Jacob snapped the reins and yelled at them, the horses took fearful, timid steps. They had to be led carefully to avoid the mounds of frozen ice.

Each step was taken with apprehension by both men and horses. The fear of falling was constant. The wagon wheels, made with wooden spokes and metal rims, made loud, shrieking sounds as they churned their tortuous way over the ice. Several times, a wheel slipped into a crevice and Jake and Corney had to take a wooden plank to lift it back onto the ice.

While the wagon was inching along, trying to maneuver around the sharp obstacles on the ice, the Neufeld family didn't realize that, just a short distance away, another family was also attempting the crossing. Later, they would learn that the Isaacs' wagon had become completely isolated when the ice cracked around them, leaving them on an island of snow and ice. The Isaacses had to use poles and boards to guide their wagon back to solid ice. It was a miracle they made it.

As the Neufeld wagon continued forward, the air was filled with tension and fear. There were strange sounds, the weather was bitter cold, and the children were frightened. However, there was no turning back. They had begun the ordeal and had to continue on.

Suddenly, there was the sound of gunfire coming from behind them. Jacob snapped the reins and yelled, "Faster, faster!" One of the horses slipped and fell to its knees. Jake and Corney quickly helped it to its feet and they tried to urge the exhausted, frightened animals to walk faster.

Some of the boys inside the wagon peeked out the back to see where the shots were coming from. It was hard to see through the fog, the mist and the darkness, even though it was daytime. After continuing on for about an hour and a half, one of the horses suddenly slipped again and went down. Jake tried desperately to get the poor creature up and as he reached around its neck, he felt a sticky liquid on his hands.

Looking at his hands, Jake knew it was blood from the horse. By the way it behaved, and the fact that it could not stand up, the boys knew that the horse had been hit by a bullet. There was no purpose in trying to get the injured animal to its feet. Everything suddenly became hopeless.

Jake cried, "Pa, what can we do now?"

As if an angel were there and taking charge of the situation, out of the darkness from behind them came another wagon, belonging to the Unruh family. The father was John Unruh and the two families were well acquainted and had been friends for many years. John Unruh drove his wagon nearby and yelled, "What's the matter?"

"Our horse is down—we can't go on!" yelled Jacob.

Mr. Unruh looked at the wagon and then at the horses. He yelled back, "We don't have much time. They're right behind us somewhere. Get on our wagon, fast!"

He and Jacob knew the extra weight on the Unruh wagon might cause the ice to break. It was a chance they'd have to take.

Quickly, the Neufelds crawled onto the Unruh wagon which was already quite full, since the Unruhs had a large family of their own. The older Neufeld boys walked along the side of the wagon. Helena was going to grab the bag of extra clothes and the bag of food, but Jacob cautioned her, "No, they'll have to stay. There's already too much weight on the wagon."

Helena insisted on one thing—she would cling to the family Bible which she had brought with her all the way from Revrovka. Somehow, she had managed to save the Bible, even through the terrible flood.

The wheels on the Unruh wagon made loud, shrieking sounds as they turned and scratched over the ice. Everyone on the wagon was holding their breath, hoping they would make the last stretch to land.

After what seemed like an agonizing eternity, the shores of China came into view. The wagon had made it. Approximately thirty minutes later they finally reached land.

Mr. Unruh, knowing that the horses could not pull the weight of the wagon up the bank, yelled, "Everyone has to get off and walk."

When they reached level ground, the women and children got back on, while some of the older children continued down the road on foot, staying as close to the wagon as possible.

Jake and Corney walked next to the wagon, always on the alert, and kept their eyes in the direction of the river, trying to see if the Red Army guards were coming after them.

On the Chinese side, off in the distance, they could see a small village completely surrounded by a wall. When they arrived at the gate, they stopped the wagon, and just stared at the Chinese soldiers stationed there. No one moved but when Jacob spoke in Russian, one of the Chinese guards hurried off to find a soldier who could speak the language.

Soon, the communication barrier was broken. Mr. Unruh and Jacob spoke to the Chinese solder in Russian, telling him they were German and were trying to escape from the Communists. When the Chinese soldiers heard this, they became friendly and told the families to bring everyone and hide behind the wall.

The Chinese soldiers had let it be known that they didn't care for the Russians, but they knew that the Russians would zealously pursue any escapees. The Neufelds and the Unruhs were told to hide and remain absolutely quiet while the Chinese hid the horses and wagon.

As the two families crouched down next to the wall, which was approximately eight feet high, they could hear the sounds of Russian guards approaching near the gate. "Open up the gate," they yelled.

The one Chinese soldier who could speak Russian, yelled back, "Why should we? There's nobody here."

A Russian guard yelled, "They have to be here. We passed their wagon a while back on the river."

The Chinese stood firm and vehemently denied that anyone had entered the gate. The Russians began to curse the Chinese and some very sharp verbal exchanges took place. Jacob breathed a sigh of relief when he heard one of the Russians yell, "Then go to hell." That was one expression that everyone could understand.

The Russians, even though frustrated, did not give up immediately. They rode their horses back and forth along the outside of the wall for quite some time. If any of the people in the two families had so much as sneezed, it would have been a disaster.

Eventually, the Russians rode off, back to the river of ice, and the two families thanked God for protecting them, and cried tears of happiness and relief. They could scarcely believe that they had really made it. What joy! They were, for the moment, free from the tyranny of the Red Army soldiers, and they were now in the friendly country of China.

Jacob and Helena had traveled some two thousand miles to reach Revrovka, in Western Siberia. Then, approximately 21 years later, with their eleven children, they traveled some three thousand miles farther to the Amur River Valley. Surviving the flood and now, the escape across the Amur, the family had traveled well over five thousand miles, most of the time in freezing temperatures, by wagon and on foot.

They had accomplished this with a large family of children and not one of them, with the exception of Marie, had been lost to sickness or accident. Jacob and Helena considered this to be a miracle from God, as they rightly should!

VIII

The traumatic escape across the Amur River in bitter cold weather was still on their minds, as the two fathers, Jacob Neufeld and John Unruh, faced the next struggle. The most immediate concern was finding a way to feed their families. They explained their plight to the Russian-speaking Chinese soldier, who consulted with his superior officers. The families were directed to go inside a large building where they could warm themselves by a wood stove. They were told to sit down at a long table where they were given hot tea and pancakes.

After the meal, the children stayed close to the stove. It was such a rare treat to feel warm after being cold for months and months.

However, their comfort didn't last long. The interpreter told Jacob that he and his family would have to move on to another destination quickly. He explained that sometimes the Russian guards returned and searched for escapees.

Mr. Unruh and Jacob conferred. "Look, Jacob," reasoned Mr. Unruh, "I have a wagon and I need to move my family to a safe place. We cannot expect to get very far if we stay together. Neither the horses nor the wagon would last very long with two families aboard."

In spite of Jacob's ambiguous feelings, he did not argue or plead for additional assistance. He said, "I understand, John, you picked us up on the Amur. You saved all our lives. We will be eternally grateful to you for your kindness. If you feel you must leave, God will take care of us. He has kept us safe so far and He will continue to be our guide and our protector. God bless you, John. Keep your family safe. We hope to see you again."

The Unruh family climbed aboard their wagon and rode off as quickly as possible.

The soldiers provided a guide for the Neufeld family as they were directed to their next destination. The guide could speak some Russian and he informed Jacob that he and his family would have to get farther away from the Russian border. With the guide leading them, the family walked for two days, farther into the countryside to a small village where they were given permission to stay.

The guide introduced Jacob and his family to a Chinese man who offered to give them food and shelter if they would work for him. Jacob readily agreed to this arrangement because, for the time being, he had no choice. His family was in desperate need of food and warmth.

The family was shown to its living quarters, a one room shack that contained a small stove. The stove would provide enough heat for the room and a place for Helena to do minimal cooking.

For six weeks, Jacob and his older sons worked, cleaning yards, repairing harnesses and bridles, and hauling firewood from the nearby trees.

In exchange, they received flour, meat and beans. Helena was able to bake bread and biscuits, and together with the beans and meat, everyone soon felt stronger. It was wonderful to have a full stomach again. In Siberia, they had been slowly starving, but after a time of having enough food, the family felt themselves being healed in body and soul.

When the Chinese landlord saw how much work Jacob and his sons had done and how Jacob had repaired the harnesses and bridles, he decided that they were worth keeping around. He generously gave Jacob some money, but Jacob had no idea how much it was worth. When he used some of it to purchase shoes at a store, he realized it was worth more than rubles. Thereafter, he encouraged the boys to work even harder, so that he could save enough to buy a wagon and horses.

In the meantime, it was necessary to talk to an interpreter about the best way to travel to Harbin, China. While living in Siberia, Jacob and Helena had learned from other German families that Harbin was a large commercial center where it was possible to obtain legal papers so that one could go to other countries. As Jacob often said, "It is my fervent hope that I might be able to obtain passage to America."

Some of Jacob's money had to be used to buy food and clothing for the family. Helena and Helen, now thirteen, were busy sewing shirts and pants to fit the boys. Everyone was in need of another set of clothes, shoes and a warm cap. The weather was miserably cold and it was no small task to provide enough warm clothing for everyone.

As soon as Jacob had enough money to buy horses and a wagon, he decided it was time to move on to their real destination, Harbin. He thanked his landlord profusely for his kindness and generosity. In exchange, the man offered to send a guide along with the Neufeld family so that they would find their way to the next village.

After several weeks of traveling, sometimes encountering danger as suspicious-looking characters prowled around near the wagon, the family arrived at Harbin on June 7, 1929. They had spent many nights in old, abandoned houses, and many others out in the open, sleeping on the ground. What a relief it was to finally arrive at their destination! However, they were astonished at what they saw.

As they entered the city, the boys were amazed and, at the same time, puzzled. Jake asked, "What kind of city is this?" as they recognized not only Chinese people, but saw a variety of nationalities and races, including many Russians.

Harbin was a large, cosmopolitan, commercial center which had attracted people from all over the world. As they looked around and saw nationalities that they were familiar with, they also saw, for the first time, black-skinned people from Africa.

To their pleasant surprise, as they bumped their way through the throngs of people, they met a German family that had also escaped from Russia. Henry and John overheard them speaking in German and quickly went over to introduce themselves.

The father's name was Heinrich Thiessen. John waved to Jacob to come over and meet the Thiessen family. The men rushed to each other and shook hands, and the ladies embraced each other, all of them aware of what the other had been through. How fortunate they were to be alive and well.

Mr. Thiessen's son, Ted, had already spotted an apartment for rent, but Jacob and Helena didn't have the money required. The Thiessens decided to take the apartment for themselves, so Mr. Thiessen instructed two of his sons to go with Mr. Neufeld and his two oldest sons to help them find a place to rent. He invited the others in the Neufeld family to come and rest at his apartment.

Having lost everything in the flood, the Neufelds were extremely poor. The Thiessens were obviously better off and could afford a few things.

As the men walked through the city trying to find a place for the Neufelds, they passed several apartments which were too expensive. Finally, on the edge of the city, there was an empty room in an old boarding house which Jacob could afford.

He moved his family into this one-room "apartment" and immediately the boys had to go out to find used furniture, particularly a bed for Jacob and Helena. They promised to work for as long as it would take, long enough to get a chair, a table and a bed. Most of the family had to sleep on the floor. Even sister Helen had to sleep on the floor next to her nine brothers.

Jacob's goal, now, was to find the American Consul's office and apply for permission to emigrate to that country. As he and Jake made their way through the chaotic city, they were amazed that it was so huge, and that there were so many different kinds of nationalities.

Before long, they discovered that there were many German families in Harbin. They, too, had succeeded in escaping from Russia and its tyranny. Since they had already become acquainted with the Thiessen family, Jacob and Jake decided to pay them a visit. Perhaps the Thiessens would know where the Consul's office was located.

Jacob was now 72 and he was beginning to lose some of his physical stamina, as well as his eyesight. He understandably tired sooner, and realized that more and more he would have to depend on his sons to run errands and conduct business for the family.

The Thiessens had become acquainted with another German family, the Dave Reimers, who had visited not only the American Consul's office, but also the Canadian, the German and South American Consul offices. Their first attempt to apply at the American office met with a negative response. The quotas for the U.S.A. had all been filled and there were dozens, even hundreds, of people waiting in Harbin to go to the States.

Jacob and Jake returned to the apartment where Helena and the others anxiously waited to hear what he had learned. He told the family, "It doesn't look good for us. We heard from the Reimer family that scores of German families are waiting for permission to leave and sail to America."

Sighing heavily, he sat down on a box in the little room. Many hours of walking through muddy streets and the prospect of continuing to live in these conditions made Jacob weary and discouraged.

However, he was a practical man. "We will have to be patient," he said. "Tomorrow, we'll send Jake and Corney to try to find more information and at least, locate the American and Canadian Consuls' offices. Then we will have to try to find work so that we will have money to buy food."

That night Helena and Jacob prayed fervently that God would help them find a way to get to America. Jacob thought about his two brothers, Abraham and Peter, living in the state of Oklahoma. He had learned this from reading a church newsletter which was circulated among German Mennonite churches in the U.S.A. and in Russia.

Jacob had no idea how to contact his brothers. He didn't have their addresses and there wasn't anyone in Harbin who could help him reach them. As he mulled over his options and thought about what to try next, Jacob recalled that his brother, Peter, had a daughter named Elisabeth, who had moved from Oklahoma to the state of California. He remembered this from reading the church newsletter while still in Siberia. Elisabeth's name was in print occasionally because she had served as a church missionary to India for many years. He wasn't quite sure where she lived in California, but he recalled that it might be either of two places, Shafter or Reedley.

As he scratched his head and tried to remember the possible location of his niece, Helena suggested, "Why don't we write letters to both of the Mennonite Brethren Churches, the ones in Reedley and in Shafter? Maybe someone at those churches will know where she lives and forward a letter to her."

Jacob's eyes lit up. "That's a splendid idea! Will you write it in German? You can write so beautifully. I will dictate it," said Jacob.

Helena quickly got a piece of paper and a pencil and Jacob began:

To my beloved niece, Elisabeth Neufeld. I am your father's brother, Jacob Peter Neufeld. I am married to Helena Julia Giesbrecht and we have ten children, nine boys and one girl in our family.

We are now living in Harbin, China, in destitute conditions and longing to come to America. We have very little food or money.

If it is possible, could someone from America write to the American Consul's office in Harbin and implore the Consul to grant us passage to America? We do not have money to pay for our passage. We pray that someone there could lend us the money and we would promise to repay the money when we arrive.

It is urgent that someone from America help us. We are finding it more and more burdensome every day. There is not enough food, not enough shelter and not enough clothing. We are just barely keeping body and soul together.

Please try to help us. God bless you.

Jacob asked Helena to write a second copy of the letter so that it could be mailed to two different churches, one to Reedley, California, and one to Shafter, California. He made sure that the correct address of the Consul's office in Harbin, and his own address, were included in each letter.

He addressed the letters to Elisabeth Neufeld, in care of the pastor of the church in Reedley and the pastor of the church in Shafter, California. Jacob and Helena had no idea if their plan would be successful, but they prayed with great faith in their hearts that the letters would find their intended destinations.

After sending the letters, Jacob found work for himself and his sons. The Chinese language was particularly difficult to learn quickly and this prevented the boys from applying for clerical or warehouse duties. Generally, the work that Jake and Corney could find was limited to weeding, raking and cleaning yards.

John, Henry and Frank had ventured out to the river that flowed through Harbin, to watch the men who were fishing. Fishing was an activity that was familiar to the boys. They watched closely to see how these men fished, what kind of pole they used and what kind of bait was used. The next day, all three boys were fishing on the bank of the Songhua River.

It was incredible how Henry could catch more fish than John and Frank, but together, they were able to bring home enough fish to feed the family at least one meal, on any day that Helena requested it.

Jacob and his sons continued to work at odd jobs, earning only enough money to buy a minimal amount of food. Most of the time, they ate rice and fish. Evidently, the Chinese diet did not include potatoes because these could not be found, even at the food bazaars. When the family had flour, Helena baked bread and biscuits which provided a delicious change.

When the fall of 1929 brought bitter cold weather, Jacob knew that it was imperative that the family have warmer coats, as well as blankets for the apartment. He decided to visit the Thiessens and the Reimers to see if they knew of a welfare office where he could get assistance. As it turned out, the Thiessens and the Reimers were able to give Jacob the necessary clothing and blankets he needed for his family. He was overcome by the goodness and generosity of his wonderful friends.

Jacob learned that there were approximately seventy German families in Harbin, all waiting for papers and permission to sail to other countries. Mr. Thiessen told Jacob that the American Consul's office was now taking applications for passage to America, but that only fifteen passports per month were being issued.

Jacob was thrilled to hear this good news and the next day, he made his way to the American office. He learned that his family's name could be added to the waiting list, but he knew that he didn't have the money to pay for the tickets. He returned to his apartment to think about this problem and how to solve it.

If many of the other German families were ahead of him on the waiting list, it would take five or six months before it would be his turn. Also, he knew the money

91

would have to come from another source: either the families there in Harbin, or, perhaps, from the people in America. If only his letters would reach Elisabeth, his niece!

*   *   *

What Jacob didn't know at that time, was that Elisabeth Neufeld had married and her married name was Elisabeth Neufeld Wall. Since she had been a church missionary to India for many years and had visited the Shafter Mennonite Brethren Church, she was well acquainted with that congregation. Her sister, Anna Neufeld Fast, had moved to Shafter and she shared her home with Elisabeth on many occasions.

The Neufeld sisters, daughters of Peter Neufeld, who was Jacob's older brother, had moved to Shafter, California, in the early 1920s. Anna and her husband had raised a large family on a farm near Shafter. Both Anna and Elisabeth were now well beyond retirement age.

After Elisabeth married Peter Wall, the couple lived in Los Angeles for a few years, and then moved to a small farm in Madera, California, to be near Peter's brother, Bernard Wall. On July 21, 1929, however, Peter Wall suffered a tragic death in an automobile accident and fiery explosion at Castaic, California. Of course, all of this was unknown to Jacob.

Even though Elisabeth owned the small farm in Madera, she felt lonely after her husband's death and began to spend more and more time with her sister, Anna, in Shafter. She found comfort and companionship there.

It was at this time that the pastor of the Shafter Mennonite Brethren Church visited Anna Fast and brought her a letter he had received that was addressed to Elisabeth Neufeld. He wondered if the letter, from a Jacob Neufeld in Harbin, China, was meant for Elisabeth Wall?

When Elisabeth saw the letter, she was overwhelmed with joy. Her eyes flew open wide and her hands trembled as she removed the letter from the foreign-posted envelope and began to read. As her eyes went down over the page, she kept saying "Oh, my . . . Oh, my . . . Oh, my! This is from our Uncle Jacob. He and his wife, with their family are in Harbin, China! They escaped! What a miracle!"

She read the letter over and over again. The sisters asked the pastor to stay and have a cup of tea with them while they discussed the letter and what to do. Tears were shed as they reminisced about their uncles and relatives. They became more and more excited as they realized that Jacob was still alive and had actually succeeded in reaching them.

The letter was an obvious plea for assistance because Jacob had written that his family had little food and was destitute. Elisabeth, Anna and the pastor immediately made plans to present this matter to the entire church congregation. Since Elisabeth had served as a missionary to India for many years, and had just recently been widowed, they were sure the church family would feel kindly toward her and would also have compassion for the plight of the Neufeld family in Harbin.

In less than two months, Elisabeth had collected enough money to pay for passage for the entire Neufeld family. The congregation of the Mennonite Brethren Church in Shafter, California, had demonstrated their loving concern and generosity by contributing the necessary funds.

Elisabeth delivered the money to the local U.S. Post Office, where she paid for a postal money order, and sent a certified letter, with the money order, to the American Consul's office in Harbin, China. Then she returned to her sister's home and began to make arrangements for the arrival of Jacob's family. Anna and Elisabeth prayed that the Neufeld family would have a safe voyage to the United States. The two sisters became anxious and excited as they anticipated the arrival of Uncle Jacob and his family in America.

IX

Life in Harbin, China, was not much easier than it had been in Siberia. The winter seemed unending and the streets, fields and shanty shacks were covered with ice and snow. Since the roadways were unpaved, there was always an abundance of mud and sludge. Work was nearly impossible to find and, as a result, there was little money for the Neufeld family to buy flour or rice. The only meat that they could get occasionally was the fish that the boys caught in the river.

Sleeping on the floor in the little apartment was unpleasant and uncomfortable, and the boys practically slept on top of one another. Helena was kept busy cutting apart old clothes and re-sewing them to fit the younger boys.

During one very low point, a terrible invasion of lice infested the entire apartment. No matter how much the boys scrubbed and washed their hair, they couldn't get rid of the pests. Each day the situation grew worse. Finally, Helena realized that she would have to shave the heads of Frank, Bill, Dave, Abe and Herman, the younger five. The apartment had to be completely stripped, scrubbed and disinfected.

Each boy had to submit to a hair scrubbing the likes of which he had never felt before. Helena mixed a concoction of vinegar, soap and an insecticide borrowed from a Chinese neighbor; when applied, it nearly took off the boys' scalps.

They ran around inside the room and then outside, crying and holding their heads in their hands. They complained bitterly for hours as their skin reddened and stung. Several of the boys, particularly Bill and Dave, developed throbbing headaches and became delirious.

When there was no particular reason for the boys to be in the apartment, Helena would tell them, "Go play outside where there is room for you to run. Get some fresh air." Herman was only two, and so Helena kept him indoors.

Often the younger boys would play running games, just to keep warm. A favorite game was a Russian version of "Kick the Can," called "Chooska." Each boy took a strong stick to use for striking a can far from the center of a drawn circle. They made small holes in the mud where they could claim home base and there was one player who was without a home base. He was "It" and it was his chore to go after the can, and return it to the circle. The object was to avoid being left off of home base and having to be the "It" player. One of the boys would attempt to strike the can and knock it far away. Then he would quickly place his stick in the home base hole and force the "It" player to fetch the can.

Needless to say, with that many sticks flying and swinging, sooner or later someone got hit hard across the shins or knees. A fight would break out and Helena would have to stop the turbulence. She'd put down her work, wipe her hands on a towel, go outside and settle the boys.

The older boys, Jake, Corney, John and Henry, were constantly combing the streets, hoping to find work, or trying to learn how to speak Chinese. Once in awhile, a Chinese man would hire them to clean up his yard and haul off trash. But with so many immigrants, work was hard to find.

Everyone in the family noticed that a peculiar, foul odor seemed to be present everywhere. The Chinese did not have a sewer system, just "outhouses," or places which were designated for this purpose. Corney and Henry discovered that, once a day, Chinese men and boys would come by these outhouses, load the feces into buckets and carry them off on small, wooden carts. The Chinese covered the fields where they grew their crops with human excrement. Very little was wasted.

The boys reasoned that this practice may have contributed to the high rate of sickness and disease, which seemed to be more prevalent just outside the city.

Suddenly they had great reason to be alarmed. The family heard that there was an epidemic of dysentery and cholera in many parts of China. Pamphlets were distributed warning everyone to boil the water before drinking it and to keep their homes as clean as possible.

In spite of all their efforts, sickness invaded the family. Several of the boys became dreadfully ill with headaches, fever and diarrhea. Helena had to make a dreadful decision. She decided that the children were not to use the "outhouse" by the apartment building. She explained to the children, "From now on, for your protection, you have to use a private container which will be thoroughly scrubbed and cleaned after each use."

Even though the process was repugnant, Helena knew she had to prevent possible exposure to the disease which could have come from the filthy outhouse.

Even with this new precaution, as soon as one child began to feel stronger, it seemed another would become ill. Before long, everyone was afflicted with either a fever or diarrhea or both.

Helena was at her wits' end. She prayed that God would intervene and spare her family. Her greatest fear was that one of the children might be contaminated with cholera, a disease which usually led to death, and the fear of cholera was beginning to create mass hysteria throughout the neighborhood.

Somehow, the family was spared and gradually, they began to improve. They had survived another terrible ordeal, along with another long, dark winter.

It was during this time that Jacob noticed that his eyesight was faltering. However, going to the doctor was out of the question. They did not know of an eye doctor in the vicinity and they had no money to pay, and so Jacob began to depend more heavily on his sons.

When the spring of 1930 arrived, it became possible to walk through the streets of the city again. Jacob asked Jake and Corney to go to the American Consul's office to see if their name was still on the waiting list and to ask how long it might be before the family could depart for America.

Jake and Corney left the apartment in the morning. It was a lonely and arduous journey across the crowded city. The streets were still covered with mud and slush from the melting snow and ice. The horses and wagon wheels had made deep ruts in the road, so it was hard for Jake and Corney to find a dry place to step and they tried to avoid getting splashed by passing wagons coming in both directions.

It took them several hours to reach the entrance of the Consul's office. They sat down outside and scraped the mud from their boots and clothes. They were nervous and had to work up courage to stand in line. There were loud crowds of people milling around inside and it seemed that everyone was talking at once in twenty different languages.

When the boys got up to the window, Jake explained in German, "We are part of the Neufeld family. We would like to know if our name is still on the waiting list and how much longer will we have to wait?"

The clerk at the window understood Jake and told him to wait while he turned around and walked into another room. After what seemed like an eternity, the man returned with several forms in his hand. As he sat down, he read in a flat voice, "All of the Neufeld family's passports have been cleared. They were paid for by a Mrs. Elisabeth Wall, who sent the money from Shafter, California, in America."

Jake and Corney were speechless. For a while they just stood and stared blankly. They were stunned. Then they grabbed each other and let out a whoop of joy.

The clerk handed Jake a stack of papers and said, "Have these signed by your parents, Jacob and Helena Neufeld. Do it properly and return them to me in seven days."

Jake and Corney could only say, "Tank you, *Danke!* Tank you, *Danke!*" as they turned and left the building.

Jake wanted to run as fast as he could, but Corney warned, "Hey, let's take it easy, it's a long way back. You could drop or even lose those papers. We need to make sure we keep them in good condition."

Both boys could hardly contain themselves as they thought about greeting Pa and Ma with the good news. Finally, they would be sailing to America. They had heard that it was a wonderful place. But what would it really be like?

When they got back to the apartment, their smiles gave them away. Jacob and Helena cried and there were hugs and kisses all around when they heard the news.

All of the children gathered close to Jacob and Helena as they looked over the papers and then they knelt to thank God. They were thankful for Jacob's niece, Elisabeth, who had received Jacob's letter and had sent the money to pay for their passports, and so they said a special prayer for her.

With the news and all of the excitement, their spirits were lifted. Discouragement and despair turned into giddy joy. Suddenly, cleaning the apartment and dusting for lice could be done cheerfully because the end was in sight. Added to this new spirit was the fact that summer had finally come and the children could go outside and play.

At last, Jacob and Helena received the news that they would be leaving Harbin on September 19, 1930.

The atmosphere in the little apartment became so joyful that, with Helena's lead, the children began to sing. She had taught them many old German hymns and this appeared to be a great time to sing together, in four-part harmony. Jake and Corney sang bass, Jacob and Henry sang tenor, Helena sang soprano, Helen sang alto, and the others just filled in anywhere they could. It was a great feeling to be singing again! It had been a long time since they had anything to celebrate and now their voices could be heard throughout the building, perhaps the entire neighborhood.

Even though they were still unable to get much food, they knew they could endure anything, now that they were leaving for America!

During the summer months, Jacob had become quite ill with a hernia problem and had to undergo surgery to correct it. He was a large man with exceptional strength and physical stamina, and he would have to call upon all of this to endure the surgery without an anesthetic. Out

100

of desperation, Jake and Corney found a Chinese doctor who was willing to help Jacob. The doctor gave Jacob a liquid to drink and this made him somewhat sleepy during the surgery.

The boys paid the doctor but Jacob considered the hernia operation to be a minor event in light of the impending departure for America. As the time drew near, and as she had done so many times before, Helena once again began to prepare a bundle with extra clothes and a sack of food for the journey.

She dressed each of the six younger boys in a shirt and pair of pants that she had sewn, cleaned on the scrub board, and ironed. The clothes were all a dark color, reflecting the Chinese influence, with a short, stand-up collar buttoned tightly against the neck, and with long sleeves tightly buttoned at the wrists. Their clothes were quite a contrast to their fair skin and sandy-colored hair.

It had been a difficult time, living in Harbin, what with the terrible smells, being sandwiched together like sardines in a small room, and very seldom having a well-balanced meal to eat. As a result, everyone in the family was undernourished.

As they walked outside of the apartment for the last time, Helena and Jacob turned around and said farewell to the little room, which had been their home for fifteen long months. They offered a brief prayer of thanks, and with a hopeful attitude, started walking toward the train station.

As they were walking, Jacob and Helena consoled each other. They had such mixed emotions. On the one hand, they were thrilled to be on their way to America, but a heavy cloud of grief hung over their hearts because of their daughter, Marie, who had been left in Siberia.

They knew all too well that she could already be suffering at the hands of the Red Army soldiers.

What a terrible decision Jacob had to make! But it was a choice of leaving Marie behind or sacrificing Jake to the military. Also, the entire family would have been in jeopardy if Jake had been arrested. Jacob and Helena would certainly have been accused of shielding a soldier who had deserted the army.

Jacob and Helena wept as they thought about Marie, their first child. They knew they would never see her again and would probably never learn of her fate. "The pain of this pierces my heart like a knife," Helena sobbed. She would carry this pain for the rest of her life.

When Jacob saw that the younger children were becoming upset at their parents' tears, he became gruff. "How fortunate we are to be leaving China and going to America. Enough crying!"

Arriving at the train station, the family checked in with the railroad clerk. Because Jacob's eyesight was now so limited, he had given the papers and passports to Jake, who was 20, for safekeeping. They each held their breath as the clerk studied the paperwork.

Finally, the clerk looked up and nodded, handing them boarding passes. Breathing a sigh of relief, one by one they climbed up the steps into the train which would take them to the coast of China and the Sea of Japan.

Bill and Frank smiled broadly as they sat down in a real train car, quite different from the open cattle car they had endured from Omsk to Blagoveshensk. Jake and several of the younger brothers stood close to the window so that they could watch the city of Harbin, gray and dirty even in the mid-day sun, gradually fade out of sight.

After the novelty of sitting in the railroad car began to wear off, some of the boys decided to take a walk and visit some of the other cars. Dave, the eight-year-old, and Abe, five years old, were interested in watching the people on the train. Suddenly they came face-to-face with a huge man who wore heavy furs and had long, shaggy hair and a black beard so dense that only his eyes were visible.

"He looks like some kind of monster," Abe whispered to Dave. For a moment they just stood there, frozen. The huge man was standing in the aisle, making it virtually impossible for them to get past him. When he saw how the boys stared at him, he suddenly lurched at them bellowing and waving his cane.

That was all they needed. They high-tailed it back to Jacob and Helena. For several nights thereafter, the boys had nightmares about the "monster man" they had seen on the train. Jacob thought that the strange man was probably also a foreigner much like themselves and just teasing the boys.

The trip took the family up over steep terrain and then on a gradual descent to the coastal plain of eastern China. There, they transferred to a small cargo ship bound for Kobe, Japan. For the first time in their lives, the Neufelds found out what it was like to sail on a rough sea. The Sea of Japan was filled with choppy waves and rolling swells.

As the tiny vessel struggled through the churning water, Helena was the first to become seasick and was confined to her bed. The older boys and Jacob felt all right but John, Helen and Henry became ill and had to return to their room. The younger brothers, Frank, Bill, Dave, Abe and Herman seemed to enjoy the ride and remained on deck to watch the action.

Fortunately, the trip across the Sea of Japan took only three days. The harbor at Kobe was a welcome sight to Helena, as well as the children. Several immigration officials were on hand when the family disembarked. These officials immediately ushered the family to the ship which would take them across the Pacific Ocean to San Francisco.

It was the *Asama Maru,* a Japanese ship capable of transporting passengers as well as cargo and many times larger than the cargo vessel that had carried the family from China to Kobe. The Neufelds were assigned two cabins for the family.

As the family walked up the gangplank to board the *Asama Maru,* Jacob could hardly deal with his conflicting emotions. Again, thoughts of Marie troubled him sorely, but he regained his composure and began to concentrate on the trip ahead of them. Soon, he thought, they would actually arrive at that land of plenty, peace and freedom—America.

Once aboard and safely in their cabins, Jacob and Helena called all the children together for family prayer. They looked at each other and many had tears running down their cheeks. Could it really be true? Were they really headed for America where people were free to live their lives without fear of soldiers who could arrest them or have them killed? Would they actually have enough food and a place to live?

At this point, things appeared to be headed in the right direction, but there was always a nagging worry that something could go wrong, and Jacob carried that burdensome thought with him continuously.

As the family was dealing with conflicting emotions, there was a knock on the door. Jacob had heard many loud knocks at doors before this and he shouted, "Who's there?"

A man's voice answered in Japanese, and, of course, Jacob could not understand what was said. Going to the door, he opened it slightly and peeked out. A printed note was handed to him by one of the Japanese ship officials. Jacob looked at the note and handed it to Jake, whose eyesight was considerably better.

The note was printed in several different languages, including German. It turned out to be an announcement telling them that it would take several days to complete loading the ship, and that certain passengers had been given permission to disembark and visit the city. It was to be the Neufelds' turn, but for eight hours only.

At first Jacob decided that Jake and Corney could leave the ship and visit Kobe. Not being able to speak Japanese was a handicap, but not being able to see very well was a much more serious matter. He decided to chance it and go along with the boys anyway.

It didn't take long for the three to find out that the Japanese people were friendly and hospitable. They wandered down one of the busy Kobe streets where people were scurrying here and there doing their shopping and sight-seeing. Many of the stores had displays of clothing and footwear just outside the store and extending into the street. Jacob had never seen such an array of bright colors before in his entire life.

As he watched the action, he was amazed at the abundance of silver, scarlet and gold-colored garments and the beautiful silk dresses and scarves. He thought of Helena. He had never been able to purchase a gift for her before. Their money had always barely covered the basic essentials like flour, wool or a cow for milk.

He felt a keen sense of neglect in this regard but he had very little money and certainly no Japanese money. Searching through his pockets his hand fell upon the pocket knife he had purchased in Harbin.

Stepping closer to the racks filled with gorgeous colors, his eye fell upon a beautiful blue silk scarf. As he picked up the scarf and began to run his fingers over it, a Japanese lady came over and spoke to him. Jacob could not understand her, but he was familiar with these kinds of situations.

He gestured to the lady with the scarf in one hand and the pocket knife in the other, moving his hands back and forth to demonstrate an exchange. The lady seemed to know what he wanted and she shouted toward a man in the back of the store.

Jacob was pleased when the man looked at the knife and nodded his head. The blue silk scarf was his to keep. He folded it gently and slipped it into his coat pocket. Tipping his head slightly in a gesture of thanks, he smiled at the clerk and turned away. How surprised and happy Helena would be! He could imagine her face when she realized that he had bought this beautiful scarf for her. Her first gift!

Jacob and the boys spent several hours walking the streets of Kobe until their feet hurt. It was time to return to the ship.

When he entered the room and saw Helena with the children, he thought of the many things she had done for them all: sewing and mending their clothes, taking care of the little ones, nursing them when they were sick, providing food for all whenever it was available, and always putting the family's welfare ahead of her own. She was a loving companion who had produced all those children.

Jacob also knew that Helena had made an awesome choice to marry him. As he thought about her life as his wife he remembered the incredible hardships she had endured. She had never had the opportunity to do "girlish" things, never had the security every woman desires.

She had been pregnant so much of the time and had to disregard her own feelings of sickness in order to care for her children. Her work literally continued day and night. His heart filled with love and appreciation as he thought that for all of that, he would now offer her only a scarf.

With an almost shy expression, Jacob looked at Helena and said, "I have something for you." He reached in his pocket and took out the silk scarf and showed it to her.

Helena stared at the scarf and began to cry. Tears ran down her cheeks as she held the beautiful blue scarf to her face. She couldn't speak.

Hugging Jacob, she managed to put the scarf around her neck. She repeatedly ran her fingers over the material. "Never have I seen anything more beautiful!" she said. "It is the first truly luxurious thing I have ever owned." She felt her heart would burst with joy. As Helena tied the scarf around her neck, she and Jacob decided the scarf would become symbolic of a new era, a life of freedom in America.

After stopping at Honolulu, Hawaii, for refueling, the *Asama Maru* sailed into San Francisco Bay 17 days after leaving Kobe, Japan. Helena and several of the boys had been violently seasick. Most of the children showed obvious signs of malnourishment.

In addition to the lack of food, Helena was ill for a different reason—she was five months pregnant with her thirteenth child. Some of the boys were embarrassed and even disgusted that Mom was pregnant again. After all, she was almost 44 and Jacob was now almost 74!

Frank wryly commented to Bill, "Well, I think Mom and Dad have certainly done their part to replenish the earth."

It was truly a miracle that Helena had lived through so many previous births. And now, in spite of the hardships of the past year, she was pregnant again.

As the ship sailed into San Francisco Bay, Jake and Corney stood on the deck and took in all the marvelous sights: the beautiful bay with ocean liners and cargo ships, the islands—Angel Island, Treasure Island and Alcatraz—all resting in the middle of glistening blue water. Small, white-capped waves reflected the sunshine. Although the family did not know the names of these places, they were fascinating to behold. They marveled at the scene before them and thought it was the most beautiful sight they had ever seen. This was America!

The *Asama Maru* moored near Angel Island, the entry port for immigrants entering the United States. The passengers were directed to line up and walk single file into a courtyard which served as a waiting area. Jacob and the boys looked back at the ship and waved as if to a real friend.

As each family stood in line, photographers re-arranged them for group pictures. Then they came to the first station where their papers were to be examined. Since most of the travelers were from Asia, the immigration official assigned to them could not speak German, and so he had to find an interpreter from another station. When a German interpreter was found, he asked Jacob where they were from.

Jacob answered, "China," without hesitation, because it was the truth.

The official then asked, "Where were you born?"

Looking directly into the official's eyes, Jacob said, "Russia."

The official had a puzzled look on his face. He said, "If you were born in Russia, you must be a Russian citizen."

Detecting a problem, Jacob said, "It is true; we were all born and raised in Russia, although we are German by nationality."

Naturally, the next logical question was, "When did you leave Russia, and from which port city?"

Being honest and forthright, Jacob said, "We left Russia in March, 1929, and crossed the Amur River into China. We lived in China until we received permission and passports to come to America."

The interpreter spoke to one of the officials in English. Jacob could tell that they were perplexed because they kept looking back at the family as they re-examined their passports.

The official called one of the clerks to the table and after conferring with him, the official spoke to Jacob. "There will be a slight delay. In the meantime, please take your family and follow this clerk to a waiting room where you will have to wait for further instructions."

The facilities on Angel Island were huge office buildings and dormitories for the immigrants. Many of the immigrants were allowed to leave the island immediately with friends and relatives, but those who had problems with their papers, or were ill, had to remain confined to their quarters.

The Neufeld family was taken to an area where they were told that they must remain until further notice. Individual cots and blankets were provided for each person. There was a community, or public, bathroom at the end of the hallway. The boys were fascinated with the bathroom facilities because they were not accustomed to inside toilets, except aboard the *Asama Maru*.

That evening one of the immigration clerks came to tell the family to follow him. They were taken to a large cafeteria where they were given a full meal and could sit down at a table to eat. Never had they seen so much food at one time. Jacob whispered to Helena, "This meal would have been enough to last several days in Siberia or China."

They had never been treated like this before, and already they were beginning to realize how nice it was to be in America.

After breakfast the next morning—once more an enormous meal—Jacob and the family were summoned to an office. The man in this office was obviously one of the superior officers, in light of the appearance of his desk and a picture of the U.S. President on the wall. Jacob tried to recognize the man in the picture, but he did not remember ever seeing him before.

In German the official asked Jacob, "Do you have any documents issued by the Russian government which granted you permission to leave that country?"

"No," replied Jacob.

"No passports or visas?"

"No," said Jacob. "Only the passports issued by the American Consul in Harbin."

The official looked straight at Jacob. "Then I have no alternative but to inform you that you and your family must be returned to Russia. You have no evidence of permission to leave that country, and all of the immigration quotas for entering this country have been filled."

Helena stepped forward, straightened her shoulders, and sternly addressed this man in German: "After everything we have been through to get here to America, we will not return to Russia. Sir, you may as well shoot us right now, because that's exactly what will happen if we are sent back." Her blue eyes met his and she never wavered.

The official stood and glared at Helena for several seconds. He had no response. He could sense her determination and he didn't want to get into a shouting match with her. He simply ordered one of the clerks to take the Neufeld family back to their quarters.

After the family had been given lunch that day, they were told that someone was there to see them. Two ladies and a man entered their quarters. More officials, perhaps? Jacob had no idea who they were.

At first they just stared. Then, one of the ladies spoke to Jacob in German: "Uncle Jacob, Uncle Jacob! I am your brother Peter's daughter, Elisabeth."

The distance melted. Jacob and Elisabeth threw their arms around each other—they hugged, kissed and cried. One by one, everyone in the family got a chance to hug the lady who had made it possible for them to come to America. Elisabeth introduced them to her sister, Anna, and Anna's husband, Benjamin, who had driven the car from Shafter, California, to see the new arrivals from Harbin.

Elisabeth insisted on being introduced again to each member of the family. She followed Jacob down the line, now shaking hands with each son and with Helena and Helen. Elisabeth took their hands in hers, looked directly into their eyes, and repeated each name several times. Overcome with emotion, she gave each one another long and heartfelt embrace.

As Jacob, Helena and Elisabeth continued to talk and to express their thanks to God for bringing the family to this country, Jacob knew he had to tell her what the immigration official had said. The news was a stunning blow to Elisabeth.

"How could this be?" she gasped. She had worked so hard to provide the money for the family to come to America. They had escaped from religious persecution from the Communists, from starvation and sure death.

Now they were facing deportation from America. Elisabeth declared, "It's impossible."

Elisabeth, never one to despair for long, told Jacob and Helena to be patient, remain cooperative and to pray. She had an idea. She would write a letter to the president of the United States. In that letter she described her personal years of service as a missionary to India. She listed the background and achievements of the church in Shafter, California. She asked the president for a special consideration, stating that if he, President Herbert Hoover, would grant permission for the entry of the Neufeld family into the United States, the Shafter Mennonite Brethren Church would take full responsibility for the family's welfare. She wrote that a home would be provided and that the family would receive physical and medical attention. They would have food, and jobs would be provided for all who could work.

To this day, no one knows for sure if President Hoover actually saw the letter and responded personally. However, the family believes this to be the case, because within one week, Jacob and Helena were told that the family had been granted permission to enter the United States. Once again, Jacob would recite, "God is my refuge and strength, a very present help in time of trouble."

Elisabeth and Anna returned to celebrate the good news and to officially welcome the family to America. Elisabeth spent time talking to the immigration officials and made arrangements for the family to stay long enough to be picked up and transported to Shafter.

Elisabeth returned to Shafter and immediately made plans to receive the family. When the paperwork and immunizations were completed, officials at Angel Island allowed one member of the family to leave early in order to assist with housing arrangements in Shafter.

Corney volunteered and even though he could not speak English, he was invited to visit Reedley and Shafter. While he was away, a group picture of the Neufeld family was taken by a newspaper photographer and the picture was published in the *Fresno Bee* on October 17, 1930. Some of the younger boys still had their heads shaved because of the lice infestation. Their clothes resembled Chinese garments.

Elisabeth had succeeded in finding a house in Shafter, and she was able to get several men to drive their Model A and Model T Fords to San Francisco to move the entire family. The family had not seen many automobiles before. What a novelty it was to climb into one of these cars that would take them to their home.

After about three hours of traveling time, Abe, who was five, turned to Helena and asked, "When are we ever going to get to that America?" The family would chuckle at this remark for years to come.

They finally arrived at their new home town and parked in front of their new home on the corner of Central and Kern Streets in Shafter, California, on November 1, 1930.

The arduous journey from Harbin to Shafter had taken approximately 42 days, including three weeks at Angel Island. The incredible journey from Sparrau to Shafter had taken almost 23 years.

Jacob and Helena called all the children together in the small living room of their new home and expressed gratitude to God for leading them all the way. Now they were finally safe and free from oppression, thanks to the wonderful people in Shafter and the generosity of the government of the United States and the president.

At the age of 74, Jacob was now faced with the challenge of adjusting to yet another strange country. He knew nothing of the customs, the people, or the government, but he felt secure that he and his family were safe at last.

Entering the U.S. at Angel Island, October, 1930
Father Jacob, Mother Helena, Jake, (Not pictured, Corney), John, Helen,
Henry, Frank, Bill, Dave, Abe and Herman (Courtesy of *The Fresno Bee*)

X

Many people of German descent, who had also immigrated from Russia, lived in the little town of Shafter. They had similar religious beliefs and backgrounds, and so a common bond between the Neufelds and their neighbors was easily established.

Members of the Mennonite Brethren Church in Shafter donated furniture, bedding, clothes and food for the new arrivals. Men in the church made sure there was work for the Neufeld boys, and when spring came, there was an abundance of jobs in the fields and potato packing sheds.

Learning to speak English became a natural part of working and living in Shafter. The younger boys, Frank, Bill, Dave and Abe, were sent to Richland Elementary School where they learned English and much about the social aspects of living in America.

Three months after the family arrived in Shafter, Helena gave birth to her thirteenth child, a baby boy whom she named after the President of the United States, Herbert Hoover. She wanted to do this to honor the man who made it possible for the family to enter her new country.

The older brothers were embarrassed when they came home from church on February 8, 1931, to find another baby brother in a bassinet. They were becoming aware of social practices and customs in the new country, and having children at Jacob's (74) and Helena's (44) ages was not an ordinary way of life in America. Some of the boys let their feelings show, but Helena was not embarrassed. She was very proud of her children and was convinced that each one was a gift from God.

The United States, along with many other countries, was in the throes of the Great Depression. Except for the abundance of field and seasonal farm work, other employment was hard to find. People were becoming despondent because of the slow economy. The future did not look bright. Some of the older Neufeld brothers—Jake, Corney and John—were able to hang on to menial-type work in the off-season, but gradually, the family's needs began to grow and income became less. Something had to be done.

Elisabeth had been keeping in touch with the family and she recognized their needs. She lived alone on a 27-acre farm in Madera, California, and came to Jacob and Helena one day with another idea. She wondered what the Neufelds would do if she offered to sell the farm to them. The farm would, at least, provide a place to raise chickens, pigs, and a few milk cows. Also, she reflected, "It would certainly provide a better environment to raise a large family of boys. That many boys need a whole lot more space than a small house in the city."

In 1933, Elisabeth sold the 27-acre farm to Jacob and Helena for $3,000. The balance due was to be paid in annual installments, a percentage of the profit made from raising crops. There was no down payment requested, largely because the Neufeld family had no savings.

Maybe Elisabeth Neufeld Wall should have changed her name to "Angel Elisabeth," Jacob thought. She had gone out of her way time and time again to help him and his family.

The new address in Madera was Route 1, Box 227. The elementary school, about one-half mile west of the farm, was called Dixieland Grammar School. On the crossroad next to the farm, there was a tiny gas station and market called "Kelly's Store." This area and neighborhood, together with the church, became the Neufelds' new world.

Just to the east of the farm lived the Massolinis, an immigrant Italian family with whom the Neufelds became good friends. The father and mother did not speak English and neither did Jacob and Helena. It was up to the children to find a way of communication, although some members of both families had already learned enough basic vocabulary to get by.

There happened to be a Mennonite Brethren Church about 200 yards from Dixieland Grammar School; so, of course, the Neufelds began attending services there. The minister lived with his family on a farm about one-half mile east of the Neufeld farm. The Neufelds became close friends with the Wall family and in later years, this friendship would produce two marriages: John Wall, Bernard's son, married Helen Neufeld, and Henry Neufeld, Jacob's son, married Helen Wall.

Surrounding the Neufeld farm, both to the east and west, were families with names such as: Wall, Schroeder, Wiens, Harbart, Wiebe, Janzen and Fachner. All of these families, and others, became closely acquainted with each other as they worshipped together in Sunday school and church, sang in the choir, and on many occasions, enjoyed plentiful German food at picnics and potlucks.

The 27-acre farm acquired by Jacob and Helena could possibly have become a successful venture, but there were so many obstacles to overcome! They knew how to milk cows, and the sale of milk to the creamery was a life-saving source of income. The chickens and pigs provided food for the table, but it was an unusually large table, which required more food than could be produced.

Planting and cultivating cotton were foreign concepts to Jacob and his boys, but they learned from watching and copying their neighbors. They had two horses, Tom and Maude, to pull the wagon and the plow. However, their tools and the methods available to them were antiquated and insufficient for the task. They not only had to watch what their neighbors did, but also had to ask if they could borrow the neighbors' equipment to do the same thing.

On the one hand it was difficult to raise good money crops, but on the other, after all their strife, it was good to grow a garden of vegetables and to have cows, chickens, pigs, a pasture, and some acreage in alfalfa for animal feed.

The cows produced the greatest source of income, but in a Depression economy, it became apparent that the farm would not sustain a family of thirteen.

Jake and Corney found jobs, working for other farmers in the surrounding area. John was able to get on as a truck driver. Henry was an irrigator for some of the neighbors, but he decided to look for work in Fresno, California. Eventually, he found employment in a large hotel, working in the kitchen, washing dishes, cleaning tables and, later, as a hotel clerk at the Hughes Hotel.

Helen became a house maid working in the home of a medical doctor in San Francisco. The other boys remained on the farm, doing the best they could.

In 1933, Jacob and Helena buried their fourteenth child, a stillborn baby girl, on the farm where they lived. Helena was greatly saddened by the loss of her oldest child, Marie, who had been left in Siberia; her first-born son, Jacob, who had died at the young age of one; and now, her last child, a girl she named Clara. But, as always, life continued.

People from the church were kind and generous. They brought furniture, clothing, bedding and food to help the Neufelds. Each boy had something to wear, even if the clothes were too large and outdated. I (the youngest boy, Herb) remember the large overalls. Mother had to cut most of the material out to make them smaller and still had to put safety pins all over the place just so I wouldn't run out of them.

It seemed to me that my brother, Herman, four years older, always got the things that I wanted. When our neighbors brought us their children's outgrown clothes, we were happy to get them, but, as a child, it seemed I got the worst of the selection.

Our house, which had only thin, pine boards nailed to each side of the studs, had three rooms. There was an attic, a basement and a small bedroom which had a door to the outside only. It was probably used as a store room before we moved there. The kitchen was just large enough for a long table and twelve chairs. There was hardly enough room for Mom to prepare the meals. The living room was tiny and sometimes we moved into this room to eat so that we wouldn't bump elbows.

We had one large room where most of my brothers slept. The oldest two, Jake and Corney, slept in the tiny room on one corner of the house, which was their private domain. If anyone else even tried to sleep in there, they quickly regretted it.

Since it was so crowded with seven boys in one room, very often one of them, usually Frank or Bill, would find another spot, most of the time in the living room or outside on the porch. I had the dubious privilege of sleeping in one bed with two others, usually Abe and Herman. Of course, I always had to be in the middle. As boys will, we would frequently push or tickle the one next to us in order to get a better position or more space. It was never long before this would lead to a rip-roaring scuffle and Mom would have to settle us down.

My sister, Helen, had been smart enough to avoid these accommodations by getting the job in San Francisco. She declared, "I have no desire to sleep in a house full of boys where there's no privacy." She had enough of that.

I remember many times wishing I could do the same; get away from that farm and that crowded house.

My dad, Jacob, was almost blind by now, and my mother was hard pressed to do all of the required work; preparing food, sewing and cleaning clothes, chores both inside and out of the house. She also had assumed the impossible task of controlling and disciplining ten boys.

When I was about four, I sat between Jake and Corney at meal time. They were to keep an eye on me and make sure I ate my food. Often, the food was parcelled out carefully so that each one would get a slice of bread and some spread. Mom saved lard and gravy from all the meals and we would spread a thin layer of this on our bread, sprinkle on a little salt and pepper, and it became quite edible. When you're hungry enough, even a slice of bread with lard can taste good.

I remember one evening when each brother was given one boiled egg (and only one) for supper. I just sat there and stared at that egg in front of me. After awhile, Jake cut the egg in half and sternly told me, "Now you eat that egg or else!"

I knew what "or else" meant and so I slowly dipped my spoon into the egg and put it into my mouth. I gagged a few times but I was glad that I was so hungry because that made it go down a little easier.

It became my duty to take care of the chickens. If it hadn't been for those chickens and the cows, I don't know how we would have made it.

The two cows that came with the farm gave us enough milk to satisfy ten hungry boys, but we soon learned we needed more cows in order to send milk to the Chowchilla Creamery. Jake and Corney went on foot to other nearby farms to negotiate trades for heifers. They would offer labor in return for a young heifer or even a young pig. They knew it would take several months of hard labor to pay for a single animal, but without money, bartering was our only way.

On one day, Corney brought home a very tiny pig which had been separated from its mother. He had received the piglet from Mr. Massolini, our neighbor. Mr. Massolini had inadvertently sold the mother pig because he didn't understand English very well. We had to borrow a baby bottle with a small nipple to keep our new arrival alive. It became my duty also to care for him and make sure he got his rightful share of warm milk. At night, he would snuggle into my dad's slipper and sleep there as long as he could, or until my dad needed the slipper.

I was about seven now and so I was assigned to take care of our new guest. I asked Mom if I could have him as my very own. She gave me a vague "I guess so" answer, and I took that as a "yes." I considered the tiny pig to be mine, and so I named him "Tony." Little did I realize that I was raising him to be butchered and eaten by my own family.

The need for food was great and I had some sympathy for the family's needs, but my older brothers were more accustomed to raising animals and killing them for food. I was not. It was no problem for them to slaughter

Tony and dismember his body. I stood there horrified, then covered my eyes and ran into the house.

In my mind, the thought of losing Tony was terrible enough, but then it got much worse. Frank and Henry yelled to me, "Come out here. We've got a job for you."

Reluctantly, I went outside and there in a large, round tub was Tony's head. Frank demanded, "Pour hot water in this tub and start scraping the hair off the face and head."

I thought of running away, but I knew my brothers could easily catch me, and that would make matters worse. I started to scrape the hair, with tears running down my face while trying constantly to avoid throwing up. This was one of those times when I learned to hate the farm. I vowed that I would never eat any of the meat from Tony's body, no matter what it cost me, and I didn't.

In the evenings, it was everyone's responsibility to finish the chores, clean up and come into the living room. At about 8:30 P.M., Mom would call for us and we would gather around the table. My dad sat at the end of the table and Mom would hand him the family Bible, so that he could "read" from it. We all knew that he was too blind to see the words. Besides, we were also familiar with many of the passages that he had memorized.

The Bible, lying open in front of him, was printed in German. This was the same Bible that had traveled with Helena from Revrovka to Siberia, and from Siberia to China. It had the names of all of the children written in the family section—their dates of birth, and the dates of death of the two who were now deceased, as well as other pertinent information. This book was the only evidence we had to present to officials so that my brothers and sister, Helen, could get their birth certificates.

Mom opened the Bible to the exact book, chapter and verse that Dad requested and he would go through the motions of reading. In reality, he had the passage memorized. He had memorized hundreds of passages in the Bible, including verses in Psalms, Matthew, Mark, Luke, John and chapters such as I Cor. 13. One of his all-time favorites was Psalm 23. I always enjoyed hearing this particular chapter in Psalms because the words were like beautiful poetry. Of course, for me, the transition from German to English had to come at a later time. Jacob recited it in German.

As he quoted Psalm 23, "Yea, though I walk through the valley of the shadow of death, I will fear no evil, for Thou art with me. . . ." He would often hesitate, begin to weep, and then he would tell us of some of his experiences in Russia during dangerous and turbulent times. We heard many stories repeated about the close calls he and Mom survived.

It was from these moments of hearing my parents' stories, recalling their difficult journey from the Ukraine, to Revrovka, to Eastern Siberia, to Harbin, China, and finally to America, that I was able to learn many of the events of their incredible lives and reconstruct this chronology.

For a while, as a young boy in a large family, the impact of the stories did not dawn on me. I enjoyed hearing them, but sometimes, they made me sad. Just listening to Dad, Mom and my older brothers recall their experiences caused me to wonder how and why they were so fortunate. Why were they spared time and time again?

As I became older, I realized that they had survived against incredible odds and had never lost their faith. It was important to them to pass this faith along to the next generation. It was important to them that all of their children and children's children believe in a real God, who cared for each and every one, especially those who put their trust in Him.

Helena and Jacob Neufeld, 1939

XI

Life in Madera was full of stimulating experiences, some religious, and some far from it. Even after so long, I'm reminded how just preparing to go to church was almost a religious ordeal in its own right. Everyone had scrubbed down the evening before, and even if our clothes looked dreadful, we were generally clean.

But before we could slip into our "church" clothes, we had to take care of several chores. The animals didn't take Sundays off, so milking and feeding the cows was necessary, every morning and every evening. Usually, Frank, Bill, Dave, and Abe milked the cows and cleaned the barn. Herm and I had to feed the chickens, rabbits and pigs. All of this took at least 45 minutes to an hour.

After finishing the chores, we'd wash our hands and faces. Sometimes, it was necessary to take a quick shower. This shower was not a time of standing under warm, comfortable water. It was cold water only, under the water tank about 20 yards from the house. Like it or not, it was at least invigorating.

On Sunday morning, we must have looked like a circus act, eight boys and Mom and Dad, trying to squeeze into a two-door Model A Ford. I'm not sure how we got the Ford, but I think one of the parishioners felt sympathetic to our cause and probably donated it to the family. I knew we never had enough money to buy anything other than a few groceries.

It took two brothers to help Jacob get into the back seat. He was 250 pounds of solid weight and had to be squeezed between the front seat, which doubled up toward the dashboard, and the back of the single door. There was a huge hump in the middle of the floor where the drive shaft and universal joint were located and Pa had one leg on each side.

Mom got into the back and crashed next to Pa. The two of them took all the space in the back. Abe, Herm and I had to stand between Pa's and Ma's legs. Invariably, one of us would step on Pa's feet and he would let out a blood-curdling yell in low German, "Right on my sore toe!" I think that all of his toes had "corns" on them from a lifetime of ill-fitting shoes.

I didn't know if Pa ever used a cuss word, but his cry of pain was every bit as effective. Everyone in our family spoke what was called Low German, a dialect the family had learned from other German people living in Russia. Low German was less formal, but it was the language I spoke until I learned English at age six.

Frank, Bill and Dave piled into the front right side of the Ford, and Corncy and John took the left side. By now, the tires on that poor old Model A were taking about all the pressure they could endure.

When we arrived at church, the other families gawked and laughed as one by one we crawled out of that little, dilapidated car. I'm sure we looked like the proverbial circus clowns crawling out of an old Volkswagen.

It was fun to be at church because I was able to be with my friends. I particularly liked a boy named Henry and a girl named Ruby, who were close to my age. We'd play "Tag" around and all over the church yard. I also played with Jackie and Jimmy, who were brothers, and an older boy named Frankie.

When the first day of school arrived in September, 1936, I was eager to go because I would get a chance to see all the kids I had met at church. I had on an ancient pair of overalls and worn-out tennis shoes, but I tried not to let it bother me because of the excitement of the first day of school.

The teacher, Mrs. High, greeted the class in a friendly manner, and asked us to stand for the flag salute. I stood up with the others and moved my lips, but I did not know the words. In fact, I didn't know what we were doing. I noticed that the other kids were holding their right hands over their hearts, and so that was easy. I could do that.

From there on, things became more complicated. For about one hour, I was able to emulate the other kids: take paper, pencil, crayons and books, and place them in my desk. I looked at the crayons for a long time. Wow! All those beautiful colors. I had never seen crayons before.

But then, Mrs. High gave some instructions. I'm sure she said something like, "I want the following boys and girls to go to the back of the room and arrange the chairs in a circle."

She read off the list rather quickly. Did she read my name or didn't she? About seven or eight kids got up and walked to the back of the room. I got up and did the same.

Mrs. High walked straight towards me and—I think--she said, "Herbert, do you understand English?"

I tried to shake my head up and down to convince her that I could understand her, but then she brought a workbook for me to use.

She opened the workbook and said something like, "I want you to read this story (a paragraph) and answer the questions which follow it."

I knew Mrs. High was suspicious and I knew I was in deep trouble. I couldn't understand her instructions and I certainly couldn't read the story. She was nice enough to repeat the instructions several times, but each time, I was at a loss as to what to do.

Mrs. High left the room and returned with the principal, Mrs. Dann. They looked at me and said things to each other. They came over to me and asked several questions which I could not understand. Mrs. High took me by the hand and said, what I took to mean, "Come with me, Herbert."

We went into the cloak room and there she explained to me in English that I would have to go home until I could speak and understand English. I understood the expression, "go home," and so I took my little brown bag with a half sandwich (homemade bread and bologna) and walked out of the classroom. I waved to Henry and Ruby, but I had a lump in my throat because I really wanted to stay. I tried to keep from crying as I walked home, a distance of about one-half mile.

I was only five years old but by next year I'd be six, and I'd know how to speak English. When the next school year came, I was ready. Mrs. High didn't know what she was in for. I could read any book she gave me and many times she would choose me to read out loud for the whole class. She had to tell me to put my hand down when she asked a question, especially in arithmetic, because she wanted someone else to answer the question. My mother, Helena, had made sure I was ready. This is how it happened.

Mom talked to Mrs. Wall, our minister's wife, about my problem, and my need to learn how to read and write English. Through Mrs. Wall's generosity, Helena obtained several primary textbooks and writing materials.

Mom made me sit at the dining room table and print the English alphabet, first the capitals and then the lower case, over and over.

She also obtained a number of primary reading books, and together we slowly sounded out each word, as we read each book, one at a time. Mom enjoyed this activity because she was learning to read English along with me. Sometimes, my older brothers would look over the books that I read. When they heard me mispronounce a word, they would laugh and correct me; they were proud of me for trying.

Speaking of my mother, she managed to pass all the written and oral requirements to receive her citizenship papers by the next year, when I was in the second grade. Helena could speak English as well as I could. I was very proud of her for working so hard to become an American citizen. As I think back over those experiences, once more I realize what a remarkable woman she was.

*   *   *

In the fall of 1936, the campaign for U.S. president was in full swing. Franklin D. Roosevelt was the incumbent and Alf Landon was the Republican challenger. While he was campaigning for Landon, former President Herbert Hoover stopped in Fresno, California, to make a speech. When Mom heard about this, she was determined to take me with her to see him, because she had named me in his honor.

Two older brothers, Frank and Bill, sat in the front seat and Mom and I sat in the back seat of our 1934 Ford V-8 as we drove the thirty miles to Fresno. I remember the auditorium in Fresno was huge and magnificent. We had never seen anything like it before. People kept standing up and cheering and applauding every time Mr. Hoover spoke just a few words.

We were seated at the back of the auditorium, and when Mr. Hoover finished his speech and the program was over, Mom took me by the hand. We fought our way through the mass of humanity to the front of the auditorium where people were crowding around to see the former President. We waited a long time before we could get near him, but Mom was not one to be discouraged. Finally, we got close enough to shake his hand, and in her broken English with a heavy German accent, she thanked him, over and over, for granting permission for our family to enter the United States.

Mr. Hoover looked like a congenial old man to me. He was quite large and rotund, but had a kind smile and spoke with tenderness and warmth.

Even then I wondered if Mr. Hoover had the slightest idea what Mom was talking about, but he was polite and listened to her. Turning to me, she said, "Unt dis is my baby boy. Ve named him after you. His name is Herbert Hoover."

Mr. Hoover smiled, looked down at me and patted my head with his hand. Mom thanked him again and said, *"Dankeschoen"* and *"Auf Wiedersehen."* Even though I was only five, I can still remember this incident as if it happened yesterday.

*   *   *

Our farm was situated between the Morgan farm on the west side and the Massolini farm on the east. Sometimes, I would be allowed to walk home from school with Howard Morgan, who was much bigger than I. He was

131

Herb Neufeld, five years old, on his way to meet ex-president Herbert Hoover

in the third grade. Sometimes, he would tell me how to say things in English, and he just smiled and shook his head when I would speak to him in Low German.

Howard's father, Bill Morgan, planted cotton on his farm and my brothers learned about cotton farming by watching him. He didn't have any cows, barn, or pasture.

Mr. Massolini didn't plant cotton; his farm was alfalfa and pasture, and he had plenty of cows to milk. He, his wife and daughters would milk the cows by hand and it would take two hours in the morning and two hours in the evening every day of the year.

Mr. Massolini had a son who drove a milk delivery truck. He was a handsome, dark-haired Italian everyone called Shorty. He really wasn't very short, but he was stuck with that nickname. He came by our farm each morning and picked up two ten-gallon cans of milk, which I had rolled to the road on a dolly. I would stay to watch Shorty take two empty cans off the truck and put our full cans of milk on the truck. He had to be strong to lift those heavy cans and slide them onto the truck.

One day, Shorty yelled at me, "Hey, Herby, want to ride with me sometime?" I could understand him but I didn't know very much English.

I thought, *You bet I do!* I ran home and asked permission.

My family was so well acquainted with the Massolini family that my mother trusted Shorty and she agreed to let me go. I was really excited about riding on the milk truck with Shorty. He told me all kinds of things about the people who lived on the various farms. As he came to each dairy barn, he drove the truck as close to it as possible so that he wouldn't have to carry the heavy cans so far.

When the truck was full, he drove to the Danish Creamery in Chowchilla, a small town about ten miles northwest of our farm. He let me crawl on top of the truck where I could see all of those full cans of milk. Shorty took each can and placed it on a conveyor belt, which carried it into the creamery. Then he had to move the truck further down where the empty cans returned. He knew exactly where each can had to be placed on the truck so that the pick-ups the next morning would follow the same pattern as the empty cans.

Then came the most exciting part of the trip. Shorty drove to a small café in Chowchilla where he invited me to come in with him. I had never eaten away from home before and I was a little skeptical about the café. I really didn't know what to expect. Shorty knew this, so he asked me, "Herby, how would you like to have a hamburger?"

I shrugged my shoulders and said, "Okay."

"What would you like to drink?"

"I don't care." I knew a few English words.

"Do you like coke, root beer, orange?"

"Yea, I like orange," but I had never drunk anything at a café before, or anything from a bottle. I had heard about sodas, but hadn't tasted one.

When the waiter put the plate in front of me, my eyes must have been as big as saucers. The smell of the toasted buns and sizzling meat drove my taste buds crazy. As I sank my teeth into that delicious hamburger and drank the orange drink, I thought I had never tasted anything so good in all of my life. At the age of five, I decided that life couldn't get any better than this.

Shorty Massolini was very good to me. He not only paid for my hamburger and drink, but he let me go with him several times later, knowing full well that I had no money to pay for my food. He was truly my hero and friend.

*   *   *

My brother, Herman, was ingenious and creative, and he feared nothing. His ideas sometimes got him and me in a whole lot of trouble. He liked to dig huge caves, large enough to hold two or three of us in an underground room. Since the land was flat, the dirt had to be thrown or carried a long distance. As the hole got deeper, the dirt had to be carried in cans or buckets, up a ladder and out.

He had cajoled me into helping him dig a huge underground cave next to a giant poplar tree on our property. This tree was so large that it could be seen for miles. As we dug deeper and deeper, we ran into many roots. At first they were small, but as we continued digging, the roots became much larger. However, this didn't slow Herm down at all. He didn't hesitate to think things through. With saws, hatchet and axes, he cut out the roots to make space for a large room. Some of the roots were 4 to 6 inches in diameter.

When he thought the hole was big enough, he carried pieces of wood and boards down the ladder into his new room to use for furniture.

One evening, after a few older brothers got home from work, Frank came over to see Herm's new underground cave. He was amazed when he saw how big the room was and how much work it had taken to do the job. Then he noticed something else. Sticking out of the large pile of fresh dirt were hundreds of pieces of tree roots—some larger than my neck! In fact, I began to feel sorry for my real neck. Frank was sure the tree was going to die.

Running to the house, he got Corney and the others to come and see the damage that had been done. Mom came outside, also, and even Pa struggled out with his cane.

Frank and Corney grabbed Herm so he couldn't run. While Frank held him, Corney got into Herm's face, shook his index finger at his nose and yelled, "If that tree dies, you are going to get the lickin' of your life!"

Everyone stood there in shock as they looked at the dozens of tree roots cut out of the ground. Mom and the others shook their heads in disbelief. Every day from then on, we ran out early in the morning to see if the tree was still alive. Fortunately, for Herm and me, that beautiful tree continued to live. That was the end of his cave-digging—but not his adventurous ways.

*   *   *

Herm was also aggressive and played in all of the sports at school. He was an outstanding marble shooter at Dixieland Grammar School and he could place a spinning "top" anywhere in the bull ring, a large circle drawn in the dirt. One day, when I was in the first grade and Herm was in the fifth, some kids yelled to me that my brother was hurt. I tried to get to him as soon as possible, but the teachers didn't permit anyone near.

Herm had been playing basketball and had twisted his leg between two other players, breaking his left ankle in two places. Herm lay there grimacing in pain and crying. The teachers put him in a car and took him to the hospital. Several days later he came home with a cast which covered his leg from his knee to his toes.

Being active and full of life as he was, the cast on his leg cramped his style. He just continued to run and play in spite of the cast, and sure enough, his ankle didn't heal right. The doctor had to re-set the ankle. Not once, not twice, but *three* times. Finally, after the fifth surgery, the entire ankle was replaced with a piece of his pelvic bone. This time the cast extended from his pelvic bone to his toes, essentially ending all hope of playing sports.

Herm's surgeries were paid for by the school district and by County funds. Our family did not have the money to pay and Herm was fortunate to receive good treatment. After the last surgery, he realized he would have to be more patient and wait for the proper healing to take place.

However, Herm was not the kind of boy who would sit around and read books, or quietly draw pictures at a table. He enjoyed learning to play musical instruments and so Mom found a way to get him an old, used guitar, a mandolin, and eventually, an ancient trombone. They were all someone else's worn-out instruments, but Herm had a way of working on them and cleaning them, even tuning them if necessary, and as a result, he became quite an accomplished musician. He played in the Madera High School Jazz Band. At home, he enjoyed playing the mandolin and everyone liked to hear him perform on this instrument. So even though he couldn't play sports, he found a way to succeed.

In later years, the injured ankle and leg with steel pins in them, would prevent him from entering the military service during World War II.

* * *

The driveway to our farm had a row of fig trees on each side, from the main road to the house. Beside the house, we had a water tank shed, a chicken barn, pig pen, rabbit pens and a large, old-fashioned, wooden hay barn. There was plenty of space to plant a vegetable garden and fruit trees. It was my duty to care for the trees and the garden. Watering the plants with the hose and chopping the weeds were part of my daily routine, too.

One day I was busy watering the fruit trees when Pa came sauntering over, using his cane to feel the way. His eyesight kept him from recognizing anyone and he spoke to me as if I were one of the older boys. I was eight years old and I didn't quite understand what he was saying. He obviously didn't understand me either, and so, knowing he couldn't do anything about it, I walked away from him and quietly, under my breath, I said, "Why don't you just shut up?" This was an American expression that hadn't taken me long to learn. He slowly turned and walked back to his rocking chair on the porch.

Later that evening in the house, I heard him say to Mom, "Dey young sacht mir, 'Shaddup' (That boy said 'Shut up' to me)." My heart sank. Mom came over to me and grabbed my ear. I got a terrible thrashing that night and had to go to bed without supper. Believe me, I never repeated that mistake.

*   *   *

Even though Jacob was old, blind, couldn't speak English, and was deeply entrenched in his German ways, we could occasionally see signs of his being a good sport—and his mind was still sharp. Once or twice a month, we received visitors at our church who came from Reedley—visitors who provided the church with guest speakers and who were usually of German heritage.

If the timing was just right and we had a little extra food to put on the table, Mom and Dad would invite the guest speaker to our home for Sunday dinner (noon meal).

Jacob was thrilled when one of these visitors would come invited to our house. He was always interested in their names, their relatives and lineage so that he could identify the kinship and line of ancestry. He was very good at it.

Once on a Saturday afternoon, not a usual day for visitors, my brothers and I returned from an afternoon of swimming at Milleson's pool, located 12 miles west of our farm. As we pulled into our yard, Abe spotted Pa sitting in his rocking chair on the porch, and immediately told us to be quiet and just sit there in the car for awhile.

Jacob was waiting for the usual noises, the opening and slamming of car doors and boys running into the house. This time it was very quiet and no one was coming toward the house. We sat in the car in stone silence while Jacob slowly got up from his chair, used his cane to feel his way down the steps, and carefully moved closer to the car, always squinting his eyes in an effort to see who it was.

Feeling his way, he walked around the front of the car and came closer to the door on the right side, where, incidentally, Abe was sitting. All of us held our breaths as Abe spoke to Pa in a low, reverent voice: "Vir zint bezuch fon Reedley," (We are visitors, guests from Reedley).

My brothers nearly burst out when Pa started to speak in German to someone he thought was just visiting. We could see that he was getting excited over the prospects. Abe muffled his voice and spoke back to Pa in German, and when he did that, all of us exploded in laughter.

Pa recognized that his own sons had tricked him. In friendly gesture, he raised his cane to pretend to hit Abe. He had to laugh with his sons as we all walked into the house together to tell Mom. A simple pleasure, perhaps, and a life-long memory of our family resulted that day.

*　　*　　*

Located on the front porch of our house was a door which led to the basement. We called it a trap door because it was so dangerous and could easily cause a serious accident, as Mom often warned us. As long as it was closed, it would simply be a normal, flat surface, part of the porch floor. If anyone wanted to enter the basement, he had to unlatch the door, raise it up and lean it against the building. On the side of the basement wall was a small, perpendicular ladder which had to be used in order to get to the bottom of the basement.

The door opening was about 26 inches by 40 inches. There was no other entrance to the basement and, by any analysis, there was no other logical place to build a different entrance. As my brothers and I walked over that basement door so many times, we never even gave it a second thought.

One day, Corney needed to get something out of the basement. He had occasionally slept there for privacy and because it was cool, and had left some articles of clothing there. It was about 6 P.M. when Corney came out of the basement and was making his way to the car. He was apparently leaving to visit his girlfriend, Lorena. Without thinking, he left the trap door open.

Before he got down the driveway to the car, he heard the boards crack, followed by a sickening thud. Jacob had walked right into the hole, a path that he always walked to get on and off the porch.

As Jacob hung in the opening, one arm on each side above the hole, and the rest of his body dangling in the basement, he began to scream with pain. Frank and Bill, Dave and Abe, together with Corney, came running and tried to grab his arms and shoulders, but they couldn't budge him. He was a large, barrel-chested man, and his size prevented him from swinging his legs over to reach the ladder on the wall. Also, he was now over 80 years old.

No one could crawl through the entrance to get below him and push him upward. Abe ran to the barn and got a rope. His idea was their only hope. He threaded the rope down under Pa's arms, around his back, and then repeated the process so there were several lines of ropes, rather than one which could cut and bind.

During all this time, Pa screamed, moaned and cried for help. After Abe succeeded in getting circles of rope around Pa's body, he tied a knot so that none of the ropes could slip. Pa was beginning to panic and become hysterical. It took four brothers to hold on to the rope, and slowly, inch by inch, they raised Jacob from the hole to the level porch.

Pa couldn't move anything for a while because his neck, shoulders, and arms were cramping and he was in great pain. Before the evening was over, the brothers carried Jacob to his bed, where he remained for several days. We never knew exactly how extensive his injuries were, but it was a painful and frightening experience, one that gave me nightmares for weeks.

The day after the fall, Abe teased Pa by telling him, "We thought we were going to have to call the Kerman Tallow Works to pull you out of the basement."

Jacob knew what Abe was talking about because he had seen several dead animals picked up by this company. He had to smile in spite of his pain, and he thanked his sons for helping him out of the trap door hole.

While chopping weeds in our garden one day, I looked up to see a very unusual sight. A long caravan of old cars was moving slowly past our farm. When they got even with the front of our property, they pulled off the road and parked under a row of eucalyptus trees. The old cars had chairs and mattresses tied to their tops and sides.

The scene was so fascinating that I stopped chopping and started walking slowly to the road. When I got there, a young boy, about my age, came from behind one of the cars and looked at me. He had on a worn-out pair of overalls and his hair looked like it had never been combed.

Curious, I asked him, "What are you doing here?"

"Jist restin' fer a bit. My Daddy's lookin' fer work if he can find it. What's your name?"

I sort of grunted, "Herby; what's yours?"

"Mine's Wayne. Why don't you come on over?"

When I got a little closer, I saw Wayne's father putting up a tent. In fact, the people in the other cars were busy putting up their tents, too. There must have been at least twenty families with their tents and old junkers in that caravan.

That evening, around the supper table, we had quite an interesting topic for discussion. I heard Frank say, "They're 'Okies' and they came from Oklahoma."

We wondered where they would go and where they would find jobs. My brothers had trouble trying to find jobs on local farms and they were afraid the "Okies" would take whatever jobs might be available.

Soon, rumors traveled like wildfire throughout the neighborhood. The "Okies" were resented and made to feel unwanted. Jacob and Helena had compassion for them, remembering the life-saving help they'd received from strangers, but everyone, including our family, was poor and in dire straits.

As the years passed by and the "Okie" families became established in the community, we became good friends with many of them, especially the children who attended school with us. Some of the children in the Gentry and Rogers families became strong, student leaders and demonstrated physical ability in athletics. The boy named Wayne, whom I first met when the caravan stopped in front of our farm, turned out to be one of my best friends all through school.

*   *   *

In the fall my brothers and I would pick grapes for other farmers. Picking cotton and grapes was an adventure for me although it was dirty, sweaty, hot work. We had a streamlined, mass production technique for picking fruit. We would take two rows of grapes and place the grapes on paper trays in the center of the rows.

Abe had the job of dumping the full boxes on the paper trays and spreading the grapes evenly so that the sun could turn them into raisins. It was my job to have an empty box ready for any of the cutters (grape pickers with sharp, curving knives). When anyone yelled, "Box," I gave him an empty box and carried away the full one to Abe.

With eight brothers cutting, one spreading grapes on trays and one carrying boxes, we moved down those rows like an automatic picking machine. Other pickers and the vineyard owner, himself, would come over just to see us in action.

When we picked cotton, it looked like a giant harvesting machine taking fifteen rows at a time. Several of the older brothers could pick two rows while the younger ones took only one row. I liked to pick cotton with my brothers because we would usually sing as we worked. I loved to hear four-part harmony and all of us had learned the various parts. Since I was so young, I was expected to sing tenor, the high part, and I really enjoyed it.

When we went home after a hard day's work, we would eat supper, do the chores, and then gather in the yard to sing. Jacob and Helena would join us, loving it most when we sang a few old German hymns. My parents had sung some of those songs when they were growing up in the Ukraine, and some of Helena's fondest memories were of singing in the choir there. I'm sure that our singing brought back many other memories of past events, including the flight to Siberia, living there for twenty-two years, surviving the flood and eventually, escaping to China. I can only imagine how they felt to be sitting safely on their own farm singing with their sons.

*   *   *

It was during a hot summer night that our barn, loaded with hay and containing several cows and horses, caught on fire. The fire marshal later explained that it was caused by "spontaneous combustion."

We were asleep in the house when, all of a sudden, Bill and Dave started yelling, "The barn's on fire! The barn's on fire!"

As each one of us jumped out of bed, we looked out the window to see flames shooting as high as ten feet above the peak of the barn. We slipped into our britches and ran to the barn. Dave was already on the roof and Frank and Bill were handing him buckets of water from the animal trough in the corral. Bill yelled to us, "Get in a line and pass the buckets to me as fast as you can."

Abe ran to get more empty buckets from the tank barn and when he returned, he climbed up on the roof with Dave so that he could grab the full buckets and dump them on the fire. Frank, Bill, Herm and I kept handing full buckets of water up to Dave and Abe as quickly as we could and pretty soon, the terrible flames began to subside.

About an hour after the fire was put out by the Neufeld brothers, the Madera County Fire Department arrived with a water truck. The firemen couldn't believe that the dry barn, full of hay and several animals, had not burned to the ground. Only a small section, about 20 feet by 20 feet, had burned and when our neighbors came to see the damage, they could not believe that most of the barn had been saved. I guess the old bucket brigade idea worked quite well as long as there were plenty of good hands and brothers to go around.

*   *   *

One of the games we played was started by Herman, and I'm not sure where he got the idea. It was called "Sacksucker." Herm and I filled a large gunnysack with hay and rags, and packed it until it looked like a full sack of grain. We'd take it to the road at dusk and secure it to a long, thin cord. Leaving the sack near the edge of the road, we would hold on to the cord and crawl a safe distance, at least fifty yards, back into a field. Either cotton or corn stalks would provide a great place to hide.

Sooner or later, a car would come down the road and the driver would spot the sack and think he had come across a full sack of grain. Usually, the driver had to put his car into reverse and back up to the sack. By the time he got back to the place where the sack was spotted, we had pulled it into the field and the driver would be puzzled because it was nowhere to be found. As soon as he got back into his car, Herm would yell as loudly as he could, "Sacksucker! Sacksucker!"

Most of the drivers would laugh, but occasionally, we would get one who would swear and shake his fist. Of course, being two ornery boys, we got a real kick out of that.

One time a woman drove by pulling a two-wheeled trailer behind her car. She had gone quite a distance, about 100 yards past the sack when she decided she would back up and get that sack of grain. First, the trailer curved to one side and she had to pull forward to get it back on the road. Then the trailer curved to the other side of the road, and she had to pull forward again. She persevered for quite a long time until she finally got back to the sack of "grain."

This time we left the sack right where she had seen it. She got out of her car and came over to examine the attractive-looking sack. When she got just close enough, Herm gave the cord a good yank, the sack jumped off the ground and the poor gal screamed and nearly fainted. Herm yelled, "Sacksucker! Sacksucker!" and she began to realize the sick joke that had been played on her. I don't think she was in a very good mood when she got back in her car. However, I'm not sure, because I was already on the run.

*   *   *

I imagine that all large families, especially those with so many boys, have problems with discipline and control. In our case, Jacob was too old and Helena could not possibly control so many boys, especially when there were disagreements and quarrels. Sometimes, these quarrels would escalate into real, physical fights with no holds barred.

We had a huge diesel engine and water pump by the reservoir on our farm. There were days when the engine ran smoothly, and then there were days when it sputtered and wouldn't start at all. It took all of the energy and ingenuity of Corney, John, Henry and Frank to grapple with that old diesel engine and get it going again.

One day, Henry started to argue with Corney about the wide belt needed to run from the engine to the water pump. Soon the argument turned into "shoves," but Corney was older and stronger than Hank. The shoving soon turned into punching and wrestling, and when I saw Corney reach for a small 2x4 board on the ground, I knew there was going to be big trouble.

As the two brothers wrestled on the ground, Corney was able to swing the 2x4 just when Hank's head came around. Bash! That's all it took. The fight was over. Hank lay face down in the dirt, as still as stone, bleeding from the top of his head.

My heart was pounding in my chest and I was scared to death for Hank. Corney yelled at Frank, "Get him out of here!"

Frank knelt down by Hank and rolled him over so that his face was out of the dirt. The blood from his wound was spreading over his head and face, mixing with grime.

Dave ran to the house to get my sister, Helen, who was visiting the family during a vacation from her work in San Francisco. It was a distance of approximately 150 yards from the house to the pump where Hank was lying. Helen brought several clean towels and when she reached Hank, she dropped to her knees to clean his face and to make sure he was still breathing.

Helen tied one of the towels around Hank's head. Corney was still upset about the incident, and he walked over to Hank, picked up each leg, one on each side of his own, and dragged him, with his head still on the ground, all the way to the house. Corney would not let anyone else help carry Hank. It was obvious that the other brothers did not want to argue with Corney.

Helen was incensed with Corney's behavior, and she tried, in vain, with tears streaming down her cheeks, to get Corney to leave Hank alone so that she could take care of him.

When Corney pulled Hank to the house he dropped both legs and returned to work on the pump. Helen quickly worked on Hank, cleaning his face, pouring cool water on his head and face, and inspecting the wound.

It was not obvious how seriously Hank had been hurt, but he was able to stand up and walk by the next morning. I'm sure this incident led to Hank's decision to leave the farm and to find a job in Fresno.

Witnessing events like this one was a frightening time for me. I would have nightmares of my brothers fighting, and I would wake up crying.

*   *   *

In the late 1930s, many farmers, including our neighbors, were being hit hard by the effects of the Depression. The Neufeld family was no exception. There were times when we sat down at the supper table and Pa said "Grace," but there was little food on the table. My brothers were hungry and they began to be angry and upset. What had gone wrong? Here we were in America, the land of plenty, but there was no food on the table.

The Depression Years
Back Row: Brothers Frank, Dave and Bill
Front Row: Herman, Carmen (John's wife), Abe, Herb and Father
Jacob

At one of our suppers, some nervous whispering was heard from several brothers. Bill was becoming unexplainably agitated, and Mom demanded to know what was going on.

Then, Frank let the cat out of the bag: "Dave says he's going to the World's Fair in San Francisco."

Everyone was stunned by this announcement. How could any member of our family afford to go the World's Fair, even if it was in San Francisco? Bill got up and pushed his chair backward until it fell over.

He looked straight at Dave and with deadly seriousness stated, "By God, if I have to work so that we can get by, you're not going on any trip to the World's Fair. You're going to stay home and work just like the rest of us."

Bill was 18 and Dave was 17, just the right age for being inclined to prove how strong and brave they were. Dave gave his answer: "You'll have to try and make me."

This was too much for Bill to take. He was going to teach Dave a lesson. Bill rushed around the end of the table and grabbed Dave by the shirt. Dave had been in many fights before, usually coming out on top, and he was not afraid of Bill. They began to slap and punch each other, while Mom started screaming at them to stop.

Dave lunged at Bill and they both fell to the floor, scratching, punching and kicking each other. Corney and Frank tried to separate them, but it didn't slow them down. However, the intervention served to convince the two combatants to go outside and finish the fight there.

At one point, while they were struggling with each other outside, Dave broke free from Bill and ran down the driveway and out of sight.

We did not hear from Dave or see him for several weeks. Then, one day, at noon, he came walking back to the old farmhouse, as if nothing had happened, and lay down on a mattress on the front porch. He looked fairly clean, considering the grime he had picked up during the fight. But what was even more curious was that he had a certain grin on his face and a gleam in his eye.

I asked him where he had gone when he left our house.

"World's Fair! I told you I was going, and I went!"

"How did you get there—walk?" I asked.

"I walked to the highway (4 miles to Hwy. 99), and hitchhiked my way to San Francisco. It took me awhile to get across the Bay Bridge to Treasure Island, but I made it!"

"Wow!" I said. "There's nobody around here who could go to the World's Fair. Didn't you need money?"

Dave pulled out several bills from his pocket. He waved them in my face and said, "I earned five dollars from Bill Morgan for irrigating his cotton, and I helped Ray Kelly clean out his store for a couple of bucks. And look, I didn't even use it all—I've still got some left over."

I thought Dave would be in more trouble when Bill and Mom discovered that he had earned money and kept it for himself. I couldn't help but admire him, hitchhiking from Madera to San Francisco and back, staying somewhere during the night, being gone for several weeks, and all on a few measly bucks!

*   *   *

Abe and Herman were the most "mischievous" of the brothers, and played many practical jokes on other family members. For example, one time Mom acquired a small, store-bought angel food cake, also called sponge cake. We were seated around the table when she brought it in and set it down. She smiled as she watched the expressions on our faces. Most of us had never seen this kind of cake before and were eager to taste it. It was very small, only 4 or 5 inches in diameter with a large hole in the center.

While Mom went into the kitchen to get a knife (the cake would have to be cut into very thin slices so that everyone would get a taste), before we knew what was happening, Herm grabbed the cake and in one swift motion squashed it into a ball and popped the whole thing into his mouth. Everyone gasped. We couldn't believe it, but we gradually laughed it off. Herm was in big trouble with everyone over that one—especially Mom. His disgusting behavior kept him in the "dog house" for several days after that fiasco.

*   *   *

When I was just four or five, we had a black and white spotted shepherd dog named Pat. This animal was unusually bright and had a natural herding instinct.

When it was time to round up the cows and head for the barn, my brothers, usually Dave, would tell Pat to go out to the pasture and bring them in. Pat was so eager to do this that he immediately sprang to his feet and ran as fast as he could go. He knew just how to turn each cow in the right direction and with his barking, he soon got them lined up and heading for the corral.

Pat knew each of the cows by name from hearing us yell at them. For example, if Dave would tell him, "Get Rosie, Pat, go get Rosie," we would stand at the barn and wait a few minutes, and sure enough, that beautiful dog chased Rosie into the corral. He could do this with each one of the cows.

In the evenings, Pat always sat close by my brothers as we sang and played our instruments.

Usually, in the morning, Pat would enjoy himself by going off into the fields trying to catch a jack rabbit or ground squirrel.

It was on one of these mornings that he spotted a jack rabbit and chased it into the field where Corney was mowing alfalfa. The alfalfa mower had a 5-foot horizontal blade which slid back and forth across the alfalfa, leaving a swath of freshly cut hay behind. It was pulled by our two horses, Tom and Maude.

On this unforgettable day, Corney was riding on the mower, when suddenly he noticed a jack rabbit run past the blade, just missing it. He had no idea that Pat was right behind.

Before he could react and stop the horses, it was too late. Poor Pat had run headlong into the mower blade, cutting off both of his front legs just above the knees. He was hobbling around in circles, howling in excruciating pain.

Corney jumped off the mower and ran to the house. As he spotted several brothers, he told them what happened and that he would have to destroy the animal.

When Dave heard this, he ran to Corney and begged him not to kill Pat. Sobbing openly, Dave begged, "Please, Corney, I'll take care of him—I'll take care of him!"

Corney had already retrieved his rifle when Dave approached him again, falling down on his knees, pleading for Pat's life. However, there was no possibility that Pat could have been helped. Corney knew that this wounded animal would never be able to fend for himself and there was no money to pay for medical expenses.

As Corney was walking out to the field where Pat was lying, Dave ran over there as fast as he could. He put his arms around Pat's neck, and with tears streaming down his face, he begged, "Please, Corney, don't kill him--I'll take care of him. Please, Corney, don't shoot him!"

Corney called Frank to help take Dave away from the injured animal. As Frank held on to Dave, and with Dave screaming in the background, Corney pulled the trigger. The most wonderful dog we ever had was put out of his misery. Many, many tears were shed in our family that night. We were sure that, if there were a dog heaven, Pat was surely there, probably happily herding cows and chasing jack rabbits.

I'm not sure if Dave ever forgave Corney, but in their later years, they became close friends and could talk about that terrible morning.

The traumatic events of that day affected me as a little boy, to the point where I couldn't think of Pat without beginning to cry. No one in our family ever forgot our wonderful dog Pat.

XII

The Mennonite Brethren Church in Madera, California, often teamed up with similar churches in Merced and Lodi to sponsor quarterly music festivals. Each church had a choir and several musical groups which would participate in an afternoon program. We would join together for a delicious meal that always included cold chicken and potato salad and then we'd spend the afternoon listening to, and singing, great gospel music.

On the day of December 7, 1941, when I was ten years old, congregations from the three churches met in Winton (Atwater), California, for one of these quarterly festivals. My mother and I, along with brothers Henry and Abe, attended.

During the afternoon music program, about 3:00 P.M., one of the men from the host church walked from the back of the church up to the podium. Shock was written all over his face. His lips were quivering and his hands trembling as he spoke to the congregation. His voice cracked as he said, "I regret to interrupt our program for today, but I have a sad announcement to make. This morning, at approximately 7:00 A.M., the United States fleet was attacked by Japanese airplanes at Pearl Harbor, in Honolulu, Hawaii. Many Americans have lost their lives."

He stood behind the podium, wiping tears from his eyes. Some members of the congregation began to move toward the exits. Others stood quietly and began to weep and pray. One of the pastors walked over to the podium and asked the people to bow their heads, as he offered a prayer for our country and the safety of those involved in the attack.

The somber atmosphere and grave concern expressed made chills go down my spine. Even though I was only ten, the mood of the adults affected me greatly. I felt an ominous, heavy burden come over my mind and my body. I could not imagine that our country was at war.

After returning home from the music festival, my brothers began talking about the impending battle. Franklin D. Roosevelt, our President, spoke to the nation by radio the next day, declaring war on Japan. Shortly thereafter, the United States also declared war on Germany and the Axis powers. It was immediately known as "World War II."

Although Jacob and Helena were religious pacifists and were shocked by the news that the United States was at war, my brothers began to express different feelings. Our family had struggled to escape from tyranny and oppression in Russia and had been graciously received by the United States. We were now living in a land of freedom and opportunity and were extremely appreciative and loyal to this country.

It didn't take long for "Uncle Sam" to plead his cause for soldiers to be enlisted in the war effort. None of my brothers ever expressed any opposition to being enlisted or drafted into the military service. It was only a matter of time for it to happen.

Frank was the first one to enlist. After he passed his physical exam in Fresno, it was just weeks before we drove into Madera and parked the car on Yosemite Avenue in front of the County Court House where he had been assigned to report.

The Neufeld brothers prior to WWII, circa 1941

Standing: Jake, Dave, Abe, Corney, Herb, Herman, Bill, and brother-in-law, John Wall

Front: Henry, holding his son, Billy, and John (not pictured, Frank)

Jacob was not well enough to ride into town. He was 85 at the time and his eyesight had failed completely. However, he spoke with Frank and reminded him, and all of us, about Psalm 91:7: "A thousand may fall at your side, and ten thousand at your right hand, but it shall not come near you." Jacob believed that if Frank had faith, he would be protected.

Helena and several of my brothers rode to town in our new 1940 Chevrolet, the first new car our family had ever purchased. It was a real beauty for $995. All of the brothers had worked hard to earn enough to make the down payment for that car. Jake, Corney, John and Henry were married at this time and were not there to say goodbye to Frank.

At 7:00 A.M., a Greyhound bus pulled up to the curb in front of the court house. The driver and a uniformed soldier stepped out of the bus. We could hear other families talking in their cars, but when the bus arrived, everything became quiet.

As a few men began reporting to the officer in charge, the time to say goodbye had arrived. Everyone of us, especially my mother, had something to say at the last minute. Then, we hugged and said, "Goodbye" and "Good luck" to Frank. He didn't have a clue as to where he was going. He would let us know later. Right now, he just wanted to serve his country in the best way possible.

I was eleven when we waved goodbye to Frank that spring morning in 1942. Talk about ambivalent emotions! I was proud that he was going to be a soldier in the U.S. Army, but I knew I would miss him, even if he was 13 years older. He was the first brother to leave our home and enter the service. As the Greyhound bus pulled away from the curb and started down Highway 99, it was hard for me to swallow. I had a lump in my throat I'll never forget.

Several months later, it was Dave's turn. Inability to find a good job and the lingering effects of the Depression had a motivating effect on Dave's decision to join the Army. By now, Madera County had established a Selective Service Board, called the Draft Board.

First, the young men between 21 and 26 were "invited" to join the Army, Navy or Marines. If they passed the physical exam and were not working in a classified position, they were drafted into one of the armed services. At first, they drafted only single men, but in a short time, married men were required to serve.

Dave was as ready as he could be. When his 21st birthday arrived, he was anxious to join the Army and our second trip to the court house was now on schedule. Once again, we piled into that Chevy — Mom, Bill, Dave, Abe, Herm and I. It was like a repeat performance: The bus arriving at 7:00 A.M., the driver and an Army officer got off the bus and a group of young men walked forward to meet the officer.

As their names were called off, they lined up in two rows. At one point, the officer shouted a name but there was no response. Someone had evidently failed to appear. Then, the inductees were instructed to file into the bus and, again, that familiar lump in my throat began to rise.

"Goodbye, Dave. Be careful and be sure to write," I managed. I was having a hard time saying anything. By this time, we had heard the news on the radio of Hitler's attack on Great Britain and his victory over France, and we also knew of the Japanese taking the Philippine Islands.

We listened to the radio daily and heard about the atrocities committed by the Germans and the Japanese.

Red-blooded American boys by the hundreds were volunteering to join the Army, the Navy and the Marines to fight against Germany, Italy, and Japan, the Axis powers. People were buying war bonds and school children were urged to bring money to buy war stamps which later converted into bonds.

I had a special stamp book of my own. My fifth grade teacher, Ms. Stamford, made sure we all had stamp books and each day, there was an accounting. Which row of kids had brought the most money for stamps? Once in awhile someone would bring enough money to fill up a whole book. This would be approximately $18 and it would qualify for a $25 U.S. War Bond, redeemable in 10 years. What an honor.

My older brother, John, was next to be drafted. He had married his sweetheart, Carmen, and moved to Bakersfield where he worked for a house-moving company. We didn't get a chance to see him before he was inducted. We just assumed he was picked up by one of those Greyhound buses in Bakersfield.

We began to receive letters from Frank and Dave. Frank was stationed at Ft. Riley, Kansas, for basic training. Dave was sent to Texas, where the weather was hot and humid. Eventually, Frank was transferred to Ft. Benning, Georgia, and Dave was sent to Ft. Bragg, North Carolina.

Frank had volunteered to serve in the Medical Corps and Dave volunteered as a paratrooper. Both seemed to adjust to their new conditions quite easily. But then, we received word from Frank that he had a new address. He was being shipped overseas somewhere; he couldn't tell us where, but our correspondence with him would go to an A.P.O. number in New York City, New York.

After Frank and Dave entered the service, Jacob and Helena decided it would be a good idea to sell the farm and move into town. Bill was planning his marriage to Elsie, and Herman had moved to Bakersfield to live with John's wife, Carmen.

Abe and I were the only ones left on the farm to help Mom with the chores. However, Abe spent most of his time working for someone else, driving a tractor or pruning grape vines.

In the spring of 1942, I was in the field chopping weeds in our sparse crop of cotton, when I looked up and saw three men approaching me. One of the men spoke the most beautiful words I had ever heard: "Hey, son, you can put down that hoe—we just bought the farm from your folks."

I answered the man with, "Well, that sounds great to me!" I placed the hoe over my shoulder and headed for the house. I think it was obvious to the men how I felt. I couldn't get to the house fast enough to ask Mom if it was true.

Yes, we had sold our 27 acres for $3,000, the same price we had paid for it in 1933. My sister, Helena, now married and living in Madera, helped us with the details, and helped us find a house in town. As luck would have it, we had exactly the amount necessary to buy the new house—$3,000!

When my brother, Abe, turned 17 on July 4, 1942, his mind was set on volunteering for the service. The Army was accepting 17-year-olds with the written permission of their parents.

At first, Mom wouldn't hear of it, but he begged and pleaded, saying he couldn't find a job and making $21 a month in the Army would be better than nothing.

This was one of the hardest decisions my mother ever made. First of all, Jacob and Helena were Mennonite pacifists. They really didn't want their sons to fight in any war. Helena had some personal misgivings about the United States in a war with Germany. Because of her nationality, which seemed to affect her sense of patriotism, she had ambivalent feelings about sending her sons to fight against the Germans, even though she had never lived in Germany herself.

By depicting the deeds of the "Nazis" and the "Japs," the radio and newspapers were successful in inciting unparalleled patriotism in the American people. There were slogans, posters and billboards everywhere to remind Americans that we were involved in a great and terrible war. We could not sit back and take it easy. Everyone had to cooperate in helping the war effort.

Mom was finally worn down by all of the news and publicity and decided to sign the papers for Abe's enlistment. "But he is only seventeen, a baby," she cried.

Coincidentally, our minister's son, Dave Wall, turned 18 years old and was drafted at the same time that Abe enlisted. This seemed to make it a little easier for Mom to accept. Both of these young men were leaving their homes and the church where they would be sorely missed.

My brother, Bill, had married his sweetheart, Elsie Fincher, whom he met while picking cotton and grapes in the fields. His scheduled entry into the service was slightly delayed because he and Elsie were going to become the proud parents of their first boy, Johnnie.

It was especially difficult to say goodbye to Bill because we stood there, my mother and I, and Elsie, holding her newly-born baby, trying to wave and hold back the tears. Bill was the fifth brother to join the Army.

162

He was stationed in Alabama and Elsie decided to move there in order to see Bill when he could get a weekend pass from the base. While she lived in Alabama, she left her baby boy, Johnnie, with our family in Madera. It was really fun to watch Johnnie learn how to walk and say his first words. Helena was thrilled to take care of him while Bill and Elsie were away.

During the time that we were raising Johnnie, we received word that my brother, Jake, who had gone to Oklahoma to look for a job, enlisted in the Army. We found out later that he had married while in Oklahoma. I thought my father and mother were going to die of heart failue. Jake was their oldest son, the one who had been drafted by the Red Army in Russia, and had escaped. The one who had endangered the whole family when he escaped, and now he had enlisted in the U.S. Army.

Henry and Herman were also drafted, but, fortunately for them, they were sent home after failing to pass their physical exams. Henry had symptoms of a heart problem and Herman could not walk or march very far because of the foot he had broken in the fifth grade. If they had remained in the military, the total number of brothers in the service of our country would have been eight.

Corney was not drafted, but he served as a civilian-military policeman during the war. Fortunately for me, I was too young to enter the service during World War II, but my interest in the battles and progress of the war was intense.

It was really exciting when we received letters from any of my brothers. At first, the letters came mostly from Frank and Dave, but eventually, we received letters from all of them.

The letters arrived less frequently after the boys were shipped overseas. We were able to detect the whereabouts of Frank, as he wrote about the heat, the dryness and the desert-like conditions in northern Africa.

It was in March, 1943, while most of my brothers were still away, that Jacob came to the ultimate end of his journey. After a small breakfast, he decided to go outside for a short walk. Of course, being blind, or nearly so, he had to use a cane to feel his way along. At first, Helena kept an eye on him as he moved along our driveway toward the garage.

For a few moments, Helena kept herself busy in the kitchen. Then, as she wondered where he had gone, she went out the back door to find him. As she descended the back steps, she heard him cry out. He was in the garage trying to chop wood for the fireplace, had lost his balance, and fallen against a wood plank on the floor.

We found out later that the fall shattered his right hip bone into dozens of pieces. He was transferred to the hospital for the first time in his life. As he lay in the hospital bed, he told Helena, "I have escaped from many dangerous situations, and God has always helped me in the past, but this time, I fear, I have really done it. This is more than I can bear."

The next morning, at nearly 7:00 A.M., with Helena by his side, Jacob took his last breath before departing from this world.

The funeral was delayed as long as possible to give the boys time to fly home. They all made it except Frank. He was already in the African campaign and could not be sent home for the funeral.

And so the Neufeld brothers, along with their mother, Helena, and sister, Helen, said goodbye to the man who had led them out of Communist Russia to

America, the land where they had the freedom to live and worship as they chose. In the eyes of his family, Jacob was a patriarch of truly Biblical proportions.

Although Jacob did not have the privilege of seeing his boys come home from the war, each boy knew that he had received Dad's blessing and prayers for his safety.

I was twelve years old when Jacob died and during those days, my life was filled with news of the war and the devastation it was bringing to so many people.

Mrs. Banducci, our neighbor across the street, had received a telegram, "We regret to report that your son is listed as 'Missing in Action.' " Mr. and Mrs. Stephenson, parents of a friend of mine in school, received a telegram, "We regret to inform you that your son is missing in action over the Pacific Ocean." Mr. and Mrs. Justice, (Mr. Justice was the sheriff of Madera County) received a telegram that their son was lost over the Pacific Ocean.

With the news on the radio of American boys being killed in various places around the world, we thought it was only a matter of time until we would receive one of those telegrams. Mom and I talked about this possibility every day. It was constantly on our minds. Mom would wring her hands and cry every night while she was praying for her sons' safety.

During the actual fighting, we did not receive much information from my brothers. We knew that Frank was in Africa; Bill, Dave and John were in the European conflict; and Jake and Abe were in the Pacific area somewhere.

Frank and Abe were in the Army Medical Corps; Dave was a paratrooper in the 82nd Airborne Division; John was an ammunitions truck driver; Bill was a signalman in General George Patton's 5th Army; and Jake was an interpreter for the U.S. Army in the Pacific arena.

Both Dave and John participated in the D-Day invasion of the mainland of Europe. Out of a company of 200 paratroopers, Dave was one of thirteen who survived. He continued to serve in numerous air drops behind enemy lines, as U.S. troops pushed back the Germans.

On one occasion, as Dave and other Americans were fighting their way through bombed-out German cities and villages, he came upon a burning building which evidently still contained people. They were crying out for help. He stopped and listened, and then entered the burning building.

As he went inside and toward a back room, he saw a woman and two children huddled together, shivering and crying, but afraid to leave. Dave knew enough German words to let them know he was not there to hurt them, although he was carrying an M-1 rifle. He succeeded in convincing them that they would be better off to get out of the building, and at his bidding, they consented. He took the woman by the arm as she held on to the children, and began to head for an exit.

As soon as they exited the room where they had been huddled together, the ceiling crashed down, completely enveloped in flames. Before they could reach the exit, the ceiling just over their heads fell and Dave's clothes caught on fire.

He quickly pushed the woman and the children to the outside, and then threw himself to the ground, trying to put out the flames. Several U.S. Army buddies rushed over to help him beat out the flames. He was not seriously injured, just slightly burned on his right arm. At the end of the war in Germany, Dave was awarded the Purple Heart medal for this deed and the injury he sustained.

Brother John's role was equally dangerous because he had to drive an ammunitions truck carrying supplies for the American troops. In spite of the many close calls, unbelievable shelling and flying shrapnel, John was able to avoid injury. He later reported that when the trucks and soldiers were under siege, he had to stop the vehicle and crawl under the truck to hide. It was more than a minor miracle that his truck was not hit and that he wasn't blown to pieces, as the battle continued through France, Belgium and on to Berlin.

Frank was serving in the Army Medical Corps in Africa where the U.S. Army was inching its way along the Sahara Desert and eventually to Tripoli. In his letters he would describe the loneliness of sleeping in a tent, feeling the heat of the day and the cold of the night. It certainly wasn't his desire to serve in such a terrible location under such unbearable conditions.

Bill was assigned to serve in General Patton's Army which fought its way across France and Italy. He was a signalman, but he had to carry a rifle and fight just as any other infantryman most of the time. When the war was over, Frank and Bill were able to meet each other as U.S. troops occupied Rome, Italy. Previously, they had no idea where the other one was located.

At the conclusion of the war in Europe, Dave and John, also with no knowledge of where the other was located, linked up in Berlin. Both of these meetings were happy surprises for my brothers—an emotional high, especially when so many of their buddies had been killed.

One of the most amazing coincidences of all involved Jake and Abe. They had both been stationed with U.S. troops in the Pacific Ocean. However, neither one had any idea of the other's whereabouts. None of the brothers knew where any of the others were located.

After the atomic bombs were dropped on Hiroshima and Nagasaki, and the Japanese surrendered to Gen.

Douglas MacArthur, U.S. troops were dispatched to Japan and Korea to occupy those countries and maintain peace.

One Sunday afternoon, as Abe was walking with his buddies down a narrow street in Seoul, Korea, he noticed an American Jeep parked across the street. He looked at the soldiers in the Jeep, glanced back at his buddies, and with a sudden, jerking glance, he looked back at the Jeep. There, sitting in the back seat, he recognized his brother, Jake.

Abe ran over to the Jeep, screaming and yelling as loudly as he could, "Jake, it's me, Abe! Jake, it's me, your brother, Abe!"

Jake jumped out of the Jeep and the two brothers had an emotional time, just hugging, crying and pounding each other on the back.

This reunion served as a tremendous focal point for these two brothers from that day on. They really had something to talk about now, and they would be forever grateful for having their lives spared and for being able to see each other so far away from home.

V-E Day and V-J Day signaled the end of World War II. Servicemen and women were beginning to be shipped home to be discharged from the military service. Jake, John and Bill were reunited with their respective wives, events which demanded loud and long celebrations. Frank, Dave and Abe came home to our house in Madera.

The journey for Jacob and Helena, with their strong faith in God and their daily, audible prayers, had served as a guiding light to bring their sons home from a great and terrible war.

Even though Jacob was unable to welcome his boys home, Helena did her best to make up for it. She continued to lead the family with her inspirational and cheerful personality.

Returning home after serving in World War II, December, 1945
Brothers Frank, John, Jake, Bill, Dave and Abe

When all the boys and their wives returned home for a family reunion in the fall of 1945, it was the most exhilarating, joyful time in all of our lives. Jacob had completed his journey, the rest of the family was complete, and a sense of accomplishment and fulfillment was in the air.

The Neufeld Family, December, 1945
Back Row: Dave, Herb, John, Herman, Abe.
Third Row: Henry with son, Danny, Corney, Carmen, Vern, Bill, Jake. Second Row: John Wall, holding John, Jr., Helen Wall, Helen Neufeld, Lorena, Helena, Elsie, Lois, Frank. First Row: Frank Wall, Robert Wall, Billy Neufeld, Tootsie, Linda, Johnnie and Jackie

Helena J. Neufeld, 1946

Epilogue

In an effort to keep the family together as much as possible, Helena invited everyone to come to a family reunion twice a year, once near July 4th and again near Christmas.

Helena passed away in 1951, but the family continues the tradition of reunions to this day. Jacob and Helena's grandchildren and great grandchildren make a sizable group, as they gather twice a year to enjoy eating together, singing together and reminiscing. Many times the conversation centers fondly on Jacob and Helena, with someone always remembering something that was said or done "back in the old days." The heritage is a treasured one.

At the time of this writing, only one son, Herb, the author, remained alive.

After World War II, an attempt was made to locate Marie, the sister left behind in Siberia when the Neufeld family escaped across the Amur River into China. The Red Cross organization was solicited in an effort to locate Marie, but with no success.

There were two letters from Marie, which reached the Neufeld family in Madera, California, during the early 1930's. Herb was too young to understand the importance of those letters; however, it was learned that Marie had been arrested and incarcerated in a Soviet camp in Siberia. Her letters had revealed to her mother, Helena, that she was very cold and had little food to eat. As a result of those letters and the heart-breaking report from the Red Cross, it was assumed that Marie had perished in that Soviet camp, either by freezing or starving to death. Herb was the only son who had never met or seen his sister, Marie.

After World War II, all of the Neufeld brothers continued to make their homes in the San Joaquin Valley in California. Several lived in Bakersfield, one in Visalia, one in Lodi, but the majority stayed in and around Madera, where Jacob and Helena were buried.

Because there was little opportunity to gain a formal education, several of the brothers had to work at jobs which were not financially rewarding, but which provided a decent living.

Jake and Frank became meat cutters in Madera and Fresno; Corney worked for General Mills Co. in Lodi; John and Dave worked in carpet installation in Bakersfield; Henry became a distributor of butane/propane supplies in Fresno; Helen was a homemaker and mother of four boys in Madera; Bill was elected Treasurer of Madera County and served in that capacity for over 20 years; Abe was active in retail sales in Madera and Fresno; Herman and his wife, Vernn, owned and operated a general merchandise store in Ahwahnee, California; Herm was also elected to serve as a County Supervisor for Madera County; and Herb entered the teaching profession, retiring as Principal of Shafter High School in 1993.

In 1958, the number of Jacob and Helena's grandchildren was 32. By 1999, there was a total of

128 grandchildren, great grandchildren and great-great-grandchildren, a formidable group.

I was privileged to tell our family story to numerous church groups, civic organizations such as Kiwanis Clubs, Lions Clubs, veterans' organizations and others, in and around Bakersfield and Kern County. On each occasion, I was encouraged to record the story so that future generations would have an account of their grandparents and the struggles they endured.

In the Bible, generations are valuable. They are the means by which the Great Story is told. The psalmist declares, "I will utter hidden things, things from old—what we have heard and known, what our fathers have told us. We will not hide them from their children; we will tell the next generation the praiseworthy deeds of the Lord... so that next generation would know them, even the children yet to be born, and they in turn would tell their children (Psalms 78:2-6)."

There's a lot to be gained by listening to the voices of the generations that come before and after us. We see the vast number of ways God works, we are challenged by the needs, and we are encouraged by the strengths and celebrations.

I am compelled to submit the following incident which astounded me. It occurred in the fall of 1983.

During the time that I was principal of Shafter High School, I would occasionally go to a local restaurant for lunch. On one such occasion, I was sitting in the restaurant when I was approached by an elderly gentleman who said, "Excuse me, but are you Herb Neufeld?"

I could tell by his enunciation that he was German. There were still many German-speaking people living in the town of Shafter.

I answered, "Yes, sir, I am."

In a high-pitched voice, with quivering lips, he looked intently into my eyes and asked, "Do you have brothers, Jake, Corney, John, Henry, Frank and Bill, and a sister, Helen?"

"Yes, sir, I do. Those are all my brothers and my sister, just as you named them."

As I looked at this elderly gentleman, I sensed that he was a link to my family's past. It took my breath away when he said, "Well, I am John Unruh. I was on the wagon that rescued your family on the Amur River."

I stood up quickly and took his hand. I couldn't take my eyes off him, but kept looking straight into his face. The emotion was overwhelming. He was one of the children in the John Unruh family and had grown up knowing my brothers and sisters in Siberia.

I will never forget hugging that wonderful old gentleman. After all these years, I had met the only living person, outside of my own family, who could verify my family's escape to China.

Needless to say, we had a long conversation and an interesting visit. Mr. Unruh lived on a farm outside of Shafter and by a wonderful coincidence, had come into the restaurant that day.

I would like to say, "Thank you" to John Unruh and the entire Unruh family for helping my family across the Amur River in 1929. It made the difference between life and death for the Neufeld family.

Hebrews 13:2 declares, "be not forgetful to entertain strangers; for thereby some have entertained angels unawares." Angels and strangers helped Jacob and Helena throughout their entire lives.

Bibliography

Goertzen, Peggy, "The Neufeld Family of Sparrau, South Russia," a non-published, genealogical paper, Hillsboro, Kansas, July, 1989.

Isaak, Henry P., *Our Life Story and Escape,* edited and translated by Abraham Ediger and Rueben M. Baerg, Dinuba, California, 1977.

Martens, Wilfred, *River of Glass,* Herald Press, Scottdale, Pennsylvania, 1980.

Neufeld, Helena J., an abbreviated autobiography, handwritten in German script, Madera, California, circa 1939.

Neufeld, Jacob P., an abbreviated autobiography, dictated to his wife, Helena J. Neufeld, handwritten in German script, Madera, California, circa 1939.

Schroeder, William and Huebert, Helmut, *Mennonite Historical Atlas,* Springfield Publishers, Winnipeg, Canada, 1996.

Thiessen, A., "The Condition of the German Colonists in Russia," an unpublished personal account written during the 1870s, preserved by Lois Duerkson Montgomery, granddaughter, Bakersfield, California, 1996.

About the author

HERB NEUFELD was born in Shafter, California in 1931—the only Neufeld child born in the United States and the only one to graduate from high school and college (California State University, Fresno). After thirty-seven years in education, serving as high school teacher, coach, counselor, and principal, he is now retired.
He has presented the story of his family's flight to freedom to captivated audiences who have urged him to write this book. Herb Neufeld now resides in Bakersfield, California.

Address: 2000 Ashe Road, #14
             Bakersfield, California 93309

E-mail Address: herbneu@lightspeed.net

Telephone: 661-836-3812

ISBN 141208432-b